JIMI HENDRIX

THE STORIES BEHIND EVERY SONG

THIS IS A CARLTON BOOK

This second edition published in 2010 by
Carlton Books Limited
20 Mortimer Street
London W1T 3JW

10 9 8 7 6 5 4 3 2 1

First published in 2002

Text copyright © 2002 and 2010 David Stubbs
Design copyright © 2010 Carlton Books Limited

A CIP catalogue record for this book is available
from the British Library.

ISBN 978-1-84732-587-7

Printed in China

JIMI HENDRIX
THE STORIES BEHIND EVERY SONG

David Stubbs

CARLTON
BOOKS

CONTENTS

INTRODUCTION

Jimi Hendrix was, arguably, the greatest rock star of all time. Elvis Presley was the biggest seller, The King, but only those who believe that the first word in rock'n'roll was also the last would argue that the genre failed to progress following Elvis's Sun Studio recordings.

Lennon & McCartney and Jagger & Richards were partnerships: solo, they fell short of the heights they'd reached as the Beatles and the Stones respectively. Bob Dylan brought literacy and an attitude to rock music that helped drag it out of its showbizzy infancy into the 1960s proper. He may have been popular music's greatest poet (though Dylan himself argued for Smokey Robinson). Yet, skinny and scabrous, his music lacked only the sort of physical and sensual quality that the Byrds, or Hendrix himself, were able to bring to covers of his work. David Bowie and Prince were chameleons, harlequins. Meanwhile, following punk and the diversity of the post-modern, late twentieth century/early twenty-first century music scene, no single figure, or even band, has been able to dominate and even innovate in the manner of rock's ancient, legendary figures. All of the major tectonic shifts have occurred, the rock landscape is set in place, the smoke is clearing and Hendrix's legacy and supremacy are increasingly self-evident.

More than any other figure, Jimi is the magnificent embodiment of all of rock music's ambitions. His early, and not inevitable death at the age of 27 is appallingly convenient in that it freezes him at his peak, preserves his iconic status. Age shall not wither, fatten or embarrass him, nor make him resort to a bad hair weave. He remains, then as now, rock's alpha male, the man. He cut the shape and set the tone by which all subsequent "guitar heroes" were measured and generally found wanting, until finally a newer generation decided it might be wiser not to attempt guitar heroism at all but busy themselves in other musical ways entirely.

Technically, it's possible that Hendrix wasn't actually the most proficient guitarist on the planet. It's interesting, that, unlike Eric Clapton, Jimmy Page et al, he didn't really bother with the acoustic guitar. Some musos suspected him of hiding behind an arsenal of gimmicks and gadgets, of cranking up his Marshall amps to conceal technical blemishes and bum notes. Yet, when Hendrix first hit the London scene in 1966, the proclaimed rock gods of the day didn't bother to go into denial about him, or even to turn green with envy. They simply fell at his feet. They knew. When Pete Townshend and Eric Clapton arrived late at an early Hendrix show at Blaises club to check the new American guy out, they met Jeff Beck coming out, who simply rolled his eyes. Townshend asked him if Hendrix was that bad. Beck replied, "No, he's that bloody good!"

Hendrix himself never indulged in bragging and, unlike his contemporary Muhammad Ali, resisted efforts to call him The Greatest. Many who met him were surprised at how slight and unassuming he seemed in person. That's because, onstage, he projected the image of an 800 pounds behemoth.

Hendrix was a fine guitarist but, more importantly, he was a master of the new electric energy which would be unleashed across the late 1960s as

Eric Clapton – both enraptured and dismayed by Jimi Hendrix's brilliance.

rock jettisoned the "n'roll" and went supersonic. His arrival on the scene coincided with the introduction of Marshall amps, developments in studio technology and techno-boffins such as Roger Mayer, who introduced to Hendrix a welter of new devices such as the Octavia and wah-wah. Others such as the Small Faces, Cream and Frank Zappa had used these gizmos, but to nothing like the devastating effect that Hendrix did. It was as if, in terms of sonic arsenal, the music had leapt from musket fire to the thermonuclear bomb overnight. Audiences were astounded at the hurricanes of sound he hurled at them from all sides. A young Allan Jones, later editor of UK music magazines Melody Maker and Uncut, recalled seeing Hendrix in Cardiff in 1967: "The noise was terrific. It seemed to suck the air out of our lungs, left us scalded, altered."

Yet the effect was spellbinding, the noise never repellently cacophonous but sculpted – liquid and fire expertly shaped in mid-air as if by a glass blower. His working methods were a mystery, even to those close to him. Said Eric Barrett, Jimi's long-time tour manager: "If I tried to test his equipment, all I got was feedback. Jimi could control it all with his fingers, and I still don't know how he did it." Or, as George Clinton put it, "The way he could control feedback and make it sound so symphonic truly transcended logic."

Hendrix was greeted at the time as some yeti-like unknown force of nature, in borderline racist terms as a "wild man". However, as Charles Shaar Murray has so eloquently argued in his book Crosstown Traffic: Jimi Hendrix And Post-War Pop (Faber & Faber, 1989), Hendrix drew from a whole range of twentieth century musical traditions, and could be claimed by any one of them. He drew on the primal energy of the blues, his first love – he'd spent a lot of time in the deep South as a child, and learnt some of his later techniques such as how to "bend" notes, from bluesman Albert King. He earned his spurs on the "chitlin' circuit", polishing his R&B licks, learning the rudiments of funk and soul as well as the obligations of showmanship. With his penchant for free and lengthy improvisation, he admired, and was admired by, the jazzmen of the day. He jammed with blind saxophonist Roland Kirk, and would almost certainly have worked with Miles Davis had he lived. It's arguable, also, that in order to seek out Hendrix's true twentieth century peers you have to look outside rock to jazz, to freewheeling atonalists like Ornette Coleman and John Coltrane, driving themselves and their music to the absolute boundaries and expanding the known musical universe.

He also drew from less likely sources – the folk/rock of Bob Dylan, whose frizzy mane of hair he emulated, whose lyrics he worshipped and whose cracked, unlikely voice persuaded him that you didn't need sweet tones to cut it as a vocalist. He even dug the daft world of 1960s pop – he paid attention to the showmanship of Johnny Halliday and even Engelbert Humperdinck, when unwisely billed alongside the latter early on. Indeed, it was as a pop phenomenon that Hendrix was first launched on the world.

Still, Hendrix would never have been comfortable settling into any musical tradition. His roving, restless spirit made him a futurist by nature. Hence he was first drawn, for the time being at any rate, to rock music, then in its young and molten phase, a music in which the often opposite dynamics of populism and artistic innovation were – temporarily at least – married.

Emulating his warrior Native American ancestors, Hendrix used to paint his guitars before going onstage. In much the same way he was a "painter" of sound. The palate of sonic colours he drew on was immense, thanks largely to his own virtuosity, curiosity and manual dexterity (Hendrix was gifted with outsize hands and thumbs). The fact that he was left-handed but played a right-handed guitar upside-down was further testament to his ability to improvise on the instrument. It was also down to the assistance of sound engineers, primarily Eddie Kramer, who helped him realise his visions in the studio. Prior to Hendrix, and all too often after him, rock songs were set to the basic accompaniment of rhythm, melody and perhaps a fuzzy blast of guitar by way of "colouring in". The likes of the Beatles and the Beach Boys had been innovators in the use of the studio as a musical instrument, but Hendrix dwarfed both of them. With a relative minimum of instrumental and technical resources, he made music as vivid and lavishly variegated as any great classical tone poem. His songs were physical happenings – and things seemed to happen physically to those who were exposed to them. "It's impossible to merely listen to what Hendrix does," commented Frank Zappa. "It eats you alive."

Amid all this talk of the materiality of Hendrix's sound, however, it shouldn't be forgotten that, though he had to be persuaded of the fact himself, he was both a singer and songwriter. Although meandering and unfocussed as an interviewee (and probably stoned much of the time) he was responsible for coining some of the great lyrical soundbites of the psychedelic era – "'Scuse me while I kiss the sky", "and you'll never hear surf music again", "I'm gonna wave my freak flag high . . ." He ranged from monstrously metallurgical, Homeric epics like "Voodoo Child (Slight Return)", to ballads like "Little Wing" which were as exquisite as water lilies. He was as adept at chart pop as he was in forging extended soundscapes such as "1983...(A Merman I Should Turn To Be)".

A fan of sci-fi, a drifter and a dreamer, his songs weren't often full-frontally autobiographical. Yet the drift of his songs, the recurring themes, cumulatively tell the story of Hendrix, a complex man, essentially gentle and courteous yet capable of frightening, random bouts of physical violence, a constantly troubled soul who nonetheless savoured his short life to the max.

Born Johnny Allen Hendrix on November 27 1942 in Seattle, into an unstable marriage, Hendrix spent much of his childhood packed off away from home, in the care of one relative or another. He felt an empathy with the life and lot of the restless rover, like the blues men he encountered early on, whose music he revered. Racially, he drew on two heritages – African-American, plus Cherokee on his mother's side. He enjoyed dressing in

Hendrix with road manager Eric Barrett.

The young Hendrix and father Al. Hendrix Sr was a "disciplinarian", recalled Jimi, who often had to be farmed out to relatives following his parents' divorce.

Native American garb, despite the ridicule or censure he invited. The ethnic combination enhanced both his sense of individualism and of being an outsider. Like jazzman Sun Ra, he used to say that he believed he came from another planet.

You place an Oedipal construction on his relationship with his mother and father. Dad Al was a disciplinarian, mother Lucille a roving, free spirit who saw little of Jimi and died relatively young after years of alcohol abuse. He revered and longed for her in "Gypsy Eyes". However, rather than wanting to kill his father, Hendrix preferred to run away from him, while on a positive level he was well aware of his mother's failings. Girlfriends would often talk of him snatching drinks from their hands if he felt they were overdoing it. He knew what the booze had done to his mother.

Although an icon of rebellion, Hendrix himself was non-confrontational by nature. As a kid, he kept his head down. "My Dad was very strict and taught me that I must respect my elders always," he said. "I couldn't speak unless I was spoken to first by grown ups. So I've always been very quiet. But I saw a lot of things. A fish wouldn't get into trouble if he kept his mouth shut."

Throughout his life, rather than fight back, he would maintain his polite, acquiescent veneer, sublimating his feelings into his music. A perfect example occurred the night that Martin Luther King died. In a bar, Hendrix found himself sitting near a group of rednecks who cheered the TV newsflash and toasted the killer. Hendrix said nothing. The next night, however, he performed a lengthy, magnificently lachrymose and inconsolable blues improvisation to "a friend of mine" which reduced all who witnessed it to a stunned, tearful silence. It was a performance the world might have been deprived of had Hendrix got things out of his system by sailing in and whaling the crap out of those guffawing racists.

Hendrix did attempt a few agit-pop slogans late on when he came under the sway of the Black Power movement, but songs like "Straight Ahead" feel forced. Far more devastating were tracks like "Machine Gun" and "The Star Spangled Banner" in which his guitar did the talking, his fretboard a conduit for long-harboured feelings rising to the surface like a thousand howling furies, a shrieking chorus of personal and ancestral rage.

Hendrix is considered among rock's most sexually charged performers, and songs like "Foxy Lady" are near-orgasmic simulations of the pleasures of the flesh, trembling and horny. When it came to relationships, Hendrix was complex. He never wrote a song that celebrated steady love with a single, adored partner, the sort that Motown turned out by the dozen. He

regarded that sort of "love" as enslavement and preferred to be Stone Free. Hendrix did love women – he spoke of how they'd been good to him when he'd been starving on the road, and how he resolved to return as much love as he could to them. Still he was, undoubtedly, guilty of sexism. Shamefully, there were incidents when he beat up women. Yet in songs like "Angel" and "One Rainy Wish" he seems to demonstrate an almost feminized sensibility, a profound tenderness. These songs, however, were not written as hymns of praise to actual specific women but to an unattainable Ideal, a female personification of Utopia.

If one word could encapsulate what Hendrix was about, it might be "escape". He wanted some way out of here. The huge, Promethean energy of his music came from an unstinting desire to break mortal bonds by pushing back the envelope, exceeding, surpassing and outdoing the already dead and done. It would dismay him endlessly when fans called out for the old hits like "Hey Joe" and "Foxy Lady". He'd been there: he was travelling to new places. Why didn't people want to come with him? He paid lip service to notions of brotherly love and hoped his music might somehow help bring about peace. But although gregarious, there was a crucial part of Hendrix that shunned humanity. He often felt hampered by the innumerable people who wanted a piece of him. At heart he was a loner, ultimately dissatisfied by humanity, who hoped somehow to find another place beyond the Third Stone. He rapped seriously on the theme of visiting Neptune. He sang about visiting Atlantis. Though he didn't commit suicide, he dropped many hints prior to dying that he was done with Earth anyway.

Neptune? Atlantis? Hippie nonsense, you might say. However, if rock music is about questioning limits, harbouring impossible desires, then Hendrix was indeed the ultimate rock star. And no one came closer than him to making the impossible a musical reality.

ARE YOU EXPERIENCED

Recorded	October 1966 – April 1967 at De Lane Lea, CBS & Olympic Studios.
Produced by	Chas Chandler.
Engineered by	Dave Siddle, Eddie Kramer and Mike Ross.
Musicians:	Jimi Hendrix (lead vocals, backing vocals, guitar, handclaps, piano), Noel Redding (bass, backing vocals), Mitch Mitchell (drums, tambourine, backing vocals, cowbell).

HEY JOE

STONE FREE

PURPLE HAZE

51ST ANNIVERSARY

THE WIND CRIES MARY

HIGHWAY CHILE

FOXY LADY

MANIC DEPRESSION

RED HOUSE

CAN YOU SEE ME

LOVE OR CONFUSION

I DON'T LIVE TODAY

MAY THIS BE LOVE

FIRE

THIRD STONE FROM THE SUN

REMEMBER

ARE YOU EXPERIENCED

At the age of 24, Jimi Hendrix was, in sixties pop terms, getting on a bit. This was the age Ringo Starr had been when *Melody Maker* had wondered aloud in an editorial whether he was "too old to rock?" In Hendrix's case, no one had even considered the notion that he could, or would "rock", certainly not in America.

Since leaving the army, where he'd served as a paratrooper, on an honourable discharge, he'd led a peripatetic existence. His curriculum vitae showed that he'd put in sterling service in the American South on the "chitlin' circuit". There, he'd been a backing musician playing (mostly) straight R&B in the service of the Isley Brothers and Little Richard, among others. He'd earned his spurs and learned his licks. He'd acquired a sense of showmanship, but when this spilled over into outright flamboyance, he got into trouble. Little Richard, somewhat richly, had fined Hendrix for turning up to a concert wearing a frilly shirt. "I am the only one allowed to be pretty," Richard pouted.

Hendrix had booked himself a couple of recording studios and tried to do his own, wild thing. In late 1964, when he'd turned up at Stax and cut loose in a raucous, fledgling version of the sound that would later revolutionise rock music, the guys there had simply laughed at him and walked out of the studio.

The Isley Brothers – they gave a destitute young Hendrix one of his first breaks.

19

Little Richard – the wild rock'n'roller reprimanded Hendrix for being too flamboyant!

He'd acquired a little more room for expressive manoeuvre playing with Curtis Knight, who allowed him the odd solo feature, and Lonnie Youngblood. To make ends meet, he'd even recorded a one-off single with the late actress Jayne Mansfield, and gone on to form his own combo, Jimmy James & The Blue Flames. He went to New York, gravitating to Harlem, but Harlem didn't want to know about Hendrix. And so his attention moved towards where it was happening, the folk-rock orientated Greenwich Village scene. Even there, however, he found that, in the showbiz pecking order of things, as in American society at large, he was routinely expected to know his place, reduced to playing the Cafe Wha? – one of the lowest dives in the Village.

Undeterred, however, Hendrix began to grow his guitar style the way he grew his hair, using his natural physical and mental gifts, sleight of hand and quick improvisational thinking. Slight, chronically shy and almost painfully diffident offstage, Hendrix transmogrified into a colossus when given the opportunity to play. He turned the blues a hellfire red and tore the roof off the joint with his bare musical hands. Other musicians began to check out this freaky black dude who was dropping bombs down at the Wha?, from the Stones to the Monkees to The Mamas and the Papas. He became a musician's musician. But to the public, and to the industry, he continued to mean nothing. In fact, he'd developed ulcers from malnutrition combined with subsistence on methedrine crystals.

The first person to take active steps to help Hendrix realise his potential was Linda Keith, girlfriend of Rolling Stone Keith Richards. Despite her efforts, however, both Stones' manager Andrew Loog Oldham and Sire founder Seymour Stein missed opportunities to snap Hendrix up. Finally, she approached Chas Chandler, bassist with British group the Animals, who, incensed at the way naive young groups were being exploited in the rock business, was looking to set himself up in production and management.

Chandler was convinced of Hendrix' greatness. In order to manage him, however, he told Hendrix he would need him to come back to London with him. Hendrix, who travelled light through life, readily agreed. He had no serious ties in the States. There, after all, he had toiled unrecognized, one among many under-appreciated black musicians. In Britain, however, he would be a novelty. In the wake of the 1960s blues boom led by the likes of John Mayall, Georgie Fame and Eric Clapton, there was inevitably fascination at the arrival of a Real Black Bluesman in their midst.

Chandler had little option but to bring in Animals' manager Mike Jeffery, an ex-commando in the British army whom he suspected of not having cut

a square deal with his own group, as Hendrix's co-manager. He may well have been reluctant to work with a man he considered something of a shark. However, Jeffery did come up trumps when it came to difficulties in acquiring a UK work permit for Hendrix, albeit on a strictly don't-ask-how basis. He also came up with the "Experience" moniker. On the plane over, meanwhile, Chandler and Hendrix decided that, hereafter, Jimmy would be Jimi.

Once in England, the Experience were assembled. Mitch Mitchell, a young sticksman with a cocky, extrovert nature that came from years as a child actor, would be drummer. He matched the maniacal energy of the Who's Keith Moon – at any moment it was as if he was about to pitch himself right over the top of his kit in his enthusiasm. But his background was in jazz, his prime influence Elvin Jones. Noel Redding, meanwhile, was a guitarist who had had his own group the Burnettes, and had recently auditioned for the Animals. Instead, he was asked to join the Experience. His frizzy, electrocuted hairstyle, similar to Hendrix's own unkempt mop, was a factor.

Kit Lambert and Chris Stamp, who handled the Who and took a decidedly conceptual, pop-arty approach to music, signed the Experience to Track Records, who were distributed by Polydor. They saw the importance of getting the band down Carnaby Street and the Kings Road and kitted out in the foppish delinquent style of the new psychedelic scene that was turning

Greenwich Village, the Bohemian melting pot in which Hendrix developed his sense of musical identity, playing a residency at the Cafe Wha?

London from monochrome to colour overnight. It would provide an "in" to the group for curious young pop-pickers.

Hendrix was introduced to London's guitar aristocracy one by one, including Eric Clapton, Jeff Beck and Brian Jones, with whom he struck up a particular rapport. They regarded him with both awe and infatuation, occasionally mingled with wariness and even despondency. The first time that Cream, rock's first "supergroup", witnessed Hendrix, they sensed that they were about to be blown out of the water. Pete Townshend confessed that he wasn't accustomed to talking to black Americans – theirs would be an awkward relationship, with Hendrix lashing out at the Who guitarist, calling him a "honky". He perhaps felt uncomfortable with Townshend, as he had begun to emulate a few of the Brit's onstage gimmicks, including famously climaxing his sets by smashing up his guitar.

With the release of "Hey Joe" in late 1966 and an appearance on the TV rock show *Ready, Steady, Go*, Hendrix attained a public profile. He was initially regarded, if not with open racist hostility then certainly an almost zoological curiosity by the press. The *Daily Mirror* newspaper dubbed him the "wild man of Borneo", while elsewhere he was alluded to as a Mau Mau (a member of an African terrorist organization), the sort of headlines which Chandler clearly didn't discourage and probably egged on. Traditional concerns abounded at the notion of this feral, predatory creature in teen pop's midst, exacerbated by his onstage antics which included playing guitar with his teeth, exciting dangerous thoughts of cunnilingus. Mary Whitehouse, whose reactionary pressure group the National Viewers & Listeners Association certainly caught the sexual overtones of Hendrix's act, duly denounced the Experience.

Yet it was all coming together for Hendrix, from all sides. He seemed to work on every level, from the daft to the dazzling. Folk, blues, psychedelic Britpop, soul, showmanship, R&B, jazz, hippiedom, technology and sheer electric virtuosity all fed into what he was about, culminating in a fearsome and charismatic rock creature like no other. The graffiti around London in 1966 had said that Clapton was God, but this new transatlantic *übermensch* was the real deal.

Such was the sensation of Hendrix. The reality came in the Experience's debut album, in the practical difficulties they faced and overcame in making it, and in the undeniable quality of what they made.

Hendrix came to the studio armed with gadgets supplied by one Roger Mayer (fuzzboxes chained together, and so forth) as well as new, state-of-the-art Marshall amps that enabled him to send his guitar into overdrive,

Opposite: Chas Chandler, the ex-Animals bass guitarist who would manage and produce Hendrix.

Right: Mitch Mitchell of The Experience. The drummer would work with Hendrix until his death.

MITCH MITCHELL, A YOUNG STICKSMAN WITH A COCKY, EXTROVERT NATURE

THEY SENSED THAT THEY WERE ABOUT TO BE BLOWN OUT OF THE WATER

attaining a bigger, more fluid sound. Engineers were initially overwhelmed, having no idea how to process and shape the broadsides of noise that Hendrix let off in the studio. When they recorded at Olympic Studios, in the London suburb of Barnes, despite the soundproofing there were still numerous complaints from distant neighbours.

The band had been forced to decamp to Olympic following an argument at CBS's studio, which had demanded that Chandler settle the bill up to date before booking further sessions. But the Experience were living a hand-to-mouth existence, unable to continue recording for very long before having to break off and gig in order to raise the wherewithal to meet the bills. When the wolf was at the door, co-manager Mike Jeffery was nowhere to be found. Chandler bemoaned having to sell half-a-dozen of his bass guitars in order to keep the Experience afloat, though he always had an angler's inclination towards exaggeration – it was probably only two. This situation did improve when both "Hey Joe" and "Purple Haze" were instant hits, with the Experience playing *Top Of The Pops*.

One particular tour that the Experience were booked on indicated the extent to which the band were still being marketed as a pop phenomenon, as well as the unreconstructed approach of ageing showbiz impresarios towards the new "rock" music. It was a package

Noel Redding, bassist with The Experience, sharing not just a haircut but a musical empathy with Hendrix.

that included the Walker Brothers, Cat Stevens and Engelbert Humperdinck. "It was like vaudeville," recalled Mitch Mitchell. Humperdinck looked on askance at the London Astoria, as Hendrix set fire to his guitar onstage. Wary of the arsonist in their midst, the other bands gave the Experience a wide berth for the rest of the tour. Yet Hendrix was far more attentive towards Humperdinck, actually standing in the wings and taking notes on his vocal technique. Nothing was too "uncool" for Hendrix – whatever could be added to his vast range of musical reference was in, so far as he was concerned.

Gratifyingly for Chandler, Hendrix laid down tracks for *Are You Experienced* with astonishing speed. This is a tribute also to Mitchell and Redding, who were extremely quick to latch onto the sketches of songs Hendrix presented them with. There were barely any rehearsals. Arrangements were devised and carried out on the spot. There was a certain amount of fiddling with gadgets, and a shy Hendrix insisted on performing his vocal parts behind high screens. But when it came to soloing in particular, Hendrix was able to come up with the silk in no time at all.

The result was an album that is on the one hand combative and raw, on the other a measure of the rapid exponential rate at which rock was growing in the mid-to-late 1960s. It's a massive feat of both energy and experimentalism. Blues fans could get off on the likes of "Red House" – the electrification of the Delta. Sweet soul fans could drink in "Remember", acid heads could trip on "Third Stone From The Sun", rock fans get off on

HENDRIX LAID DOWN TRACKS FOR ARE YOU EXPERIENCED WITH ASTONISHING SPEED

LONDON HAD BEEN CONQUERED, AMERICA WOULD FALL NEXT

The Rolling Stones' Brian Jones, with whom Hendrix struck up a particular rapport.

the moody restlessness of "Manic Depression", while the title track exceeded the expectations of any known fan base.

And 1967 was a year of formidable debut albums. Pink Floyd's *Piper At The Gates Of Dawn* was a far more effective psychedelic bequest than the Beatles' over-developed *Sergeant Pepper*. More tellingly, The Doors' and Velvet Underground's debuts were pitch-black retorts to the sunshine hippie era. "The End" foresaw how bad it would all turn, while Warhol protégés the Velvets' spare musical approach hinted almost mockingly at the emptiness and underlying desperation of the modern age. *Are You Experienced*, however, overshadows all of these. Prior to this album, rock'n'roll was singing songs of innocence. Now Experience had dawned, a new heaviness, a de-flowering.

As would often be the case with Hendrix, critical response was either adverse (*Rolling Stone*'s reviewer adopted a studiously underwhelmed posture at Hendrix's "inane" lyrics) or, when it was laudatory, banal, as was the case with reviews in *NME* and *Melody Maker*, still both linguistically caught in the era of the 1950s UK TV pop show *6-5 Special*. In America, however, the album would benefit from exposure on the new FM radio band. Chas Chandler's plan had worked. London had been conquered, with ease. America would fall next.

(The American edition of *Are You Experienced* did not include "Red House" but did include the A and B-sides of the Jimi Hendrix Experience's first two singles, "Hey Joe" and "Purple Haze", absent from the UK edition. The CD re-release of *Are You Experienced* combines all the tracks from both the UK and US editions, and it's to this which the following text refers).

Following Page: Jimi with (left to right) Cat Stevens, Walker Brothers drummer Gary Leeds and Engelbert Humperdinck.

HEY JOE

When Chas Chandler brought Hendrix to England, he was by no means certain that his talented young charge could actually sing. The issue remained unresolved when the Experience first entered the studio on October 23, 1966, with bickering within the band as to who would undertake vocal duties, much like boys on a football field arguing about who was going to take the tedious responsibility of going in goal. Hendrix was eventually persuaded to sing, once they turned the lights right down. Hendrix was also unproven as a songwriter, and when it came to the first choice of single Chandler played it cautious, going with an arrangement by folk-rocker Tim Rose of a ready-made song, which Linda Keith had introduced to Hendrix.

Although its origins lie in cowboy balladeering in the nineteenth century, "Hey Joe" in its present form was written by one Billy Roberts, who was unexpectedly stricken by his muse on a beach in Maine and scrawled down the words to the song as they came to him with his finger in the sand. He then transferred it to paper and, unaware of the song's future value, sold on the copyright to Dino Valenti, a.k.a. Chester Powers. However, when the song became a hit, not just for the Jimi Hendrix Experience but also for Love and the Leaves, a lawyer visited Valenti in a California prison, where he was serving time for drugs offences, and extracted from him the confession that he'd played no part in writing the song. Roberts was able to collect on his royalties, but never enjoyed any similar songwriting success.

The arrangement of the song as preferred by Hendrix was downbeat and slow in tempo, giving it a heavy and haunted air. In question-and-answer form, it tells the story of a young man who, in a fit of rage at catching his "old lady" fooling with another man, shoots her and now must make his way to Mexico, and freedom. It's a song as ancient as America itself, where the notion of personal destiny generally involves moving on rather than staying and facing the consequences, putting vast distances between your past and future life. Doubtless, we're supposed to feel for Joe, whose crime is to have been betrayed and to have given vent to his passion, and who must now go "way down South" to escape the ire of the authorities, who tend to be pedantic in their insistence on bringing murderers to book.

However, to modern ears especially, the woman-done-me-wrong overtones of the song seem ugly and misogynist, with Joe's air of

31

unapologetic defiance only added to by the impromptu swagger of Hendrix's rendition. For perhaps more squeamish reasons, there were complaints when the song was eventually aired on US radio.

By Jimi's later standards, "Hey, Joe" feels tentative, only hinting at the firepower he had in store. Mitch Mitchell pounds out his authority on drums, while the bass run on the bridge adds a solid emphasis to a track whose arrangement is its best feature. Sound engineer Eddie Kramer also enjoyed the opportunity to add his own twist and touch to the recording. Only the use of the Breakaways, session backing singers whose presence was a widespread and almost mandatory feature of mid-1960s musical records, seems quaint.

When Chandler touted a demo of "Hey Joe" around the major record companies, Decca would make their second major blunder of the 1960s in passing on Hendrix, their A&R man sniffing that he was "nothing special". This was the company who had rejected the Beatles on the grounds that guitar music was on the way out. When Kit Lambert and Chris Stamp, on the point of launching Track Records, heard the song live, however, they were instantly convinced of Hendrix's greatness. The Experience's first single was also their first hit, reaching no. 4 in the UK, its success bolstered by promotion by the emergent pirate radio stations. "Hey Joe" isn't quite a leap into the future but it hints in more ways than one at a man who was on the point of crossing a major border. "That record isn't us," said Hendrix, following its release. "We only just begun."

STONE FREE

The "Hey Joe" b-side was Hendrix's first composition. With an opening chord, as if turning the ignition, Hendrix hits the road to a metronomic pace set by Mitch Mitchell. Hemmed in by a claustrophobic blues-funk, he starts to grumble. Every town he visits, he's put down by people sneering at his appearance, particularly his hair, talking about him "like a dog". This would have rung cruelly true for Hendrix when he had his first taste of British provincial towns, while touring with Engelbert Humperdinck and co. The Experience had become used to being refused admission to hotels on the strength of their appearance, their reservations mysteriously mislaid, an ignominy that would be repeated many times when they first toured Europe. Although it was probably more his clothes and coiffure that the hoteliers objected to rather than Hendrix's race, he must have been reminded of the fate of big jazz stars like Louis Armstrong and Duke Ellington, who were refused entry to whites-only hotels and forced to charter and live on private trains when touring the Deep South back in the 1930s.

However, when Hendrix embarks on the second verse, he excites rather less sympathy. "Woman here, woman there, trying to keep me in a plastic cage," he groans.

Unfortunately, he chuckles, with a roguish wink, there are times when his heart "runs kinda hot" and he's forced to scarper "before I get caught". The chorus comes complete with admonishments to womankind; "I don't want to be tied down." One wonders if Hendrix's long term and often long-suffering girlfriend Kathy Etchingham might have felt all of this was a bit rich, especially in the light of the flipside of "Stone Free". The freedom Hendrix demanded was not, it seems, one allowable to the poor, un-named girl massacred by the self-pitying Joe for her philandering. One rule for the roving Jimi, another for her indoors. This sort of hypocrisy in the supposed age of sexual liberation and emancipation for women was, sadly, so ingrained in 1966 as to not be remarked upon in its day. The equation of women with domestic stability, and therefore enslavement of the free spirit, was endemic in rock'n'roll and, before that, the blues. What seemed stone free in the 1960s seems Stone Age in the twenty-first century.

Still, "Stone Free", in its restless primitivism, is the sound of a muffled super-talent on the point of breaking out of its chrysalis. With the guitar solo, the world got the first headful of the heated aroma of Jimi Hendrix really burning rubber, while the acceleration of the fadeout is a tantalising hint at the places he could take those prepared to keep up with him.

PURPLE HAZE

The origins of "Purple Haze" are varying and confusing, not least to its author. Hendrix's girlfriend recalls that he first got the germ of the notion when he visited Speaker's Corner and the sight of a placard reading "Jesus Saves" triggered off a couplet with "Purple Haze". Hendrix himself said that the song derived from a dream "that I was walking under the sea". He later, and more plausibly, recalled that it had come from a science fiction story he had read which involved "purple death rays".

Subsequent investigations revealed that this was probably a magazine extract of Philip Jose Farmer's 1950s novel *Night Of Light*, which includes a passage about stars failing to pierce the "purplish haze" of the night sky. (The story as a whole concerns the adventures of a wife-murderer-turned-priest fleeing intergalactic justice, a curious throwback to the theme of "Hey Joe").

Hendrix biographer David Henderson ('*Scuse Me While I Kiss The Sky – The Life of Jimi Hendrix*, Omnibus, 1990) believes that purple was a colour which would have impinged itself on Hendrix's consciousness through contemplating the dusky evening skies of 1967 London, his hectic schedule leaving him at times confused, as the song has it, as to "whether it's day or night". However, Hendrix's sense of disorientation is also emotional – the song, he later explained, is "about this guy, this girl turned this cat on, and he doesn't know whether it's bad or good, that's all" – hence the line, "Is this tomorrow, or just the end of time?" which itself was uttered by Hendrix during a further bout of disorientation, when, "out of my mind" he encountered a posse of London bobbies who asked him how he was.

HENDRIX SAID THAT THE SONG DERIVED FROM A DREAM

The song came to Hendrix in a flash one afternoon though not, Noel Redding insists, an acid flash – Hendrix had, he says, yet to be initiated into LSD. Chas Chandler practically bundled him into the studio to elaborate on the basic riff he bashed out for him. Hendrix had planned to add many other verses, dealing in an epic, Homeric way with imaginary Greek-style mythologies involving the great wars of Neptune and so forth. Instead, what we have is one of Hendrix's keynote recordings, which in fewer than three minutes compresses a rumbling skyful of expression that later groups like The Grateful Dead would take (literally) hours to articulate. It's a conflation of all the myriad moments of confusion/epiphany that are explained as its origins. It impacts like a phosphorescent

burst of energy, at once blinding and ultra-revelatory. Purple was indeed the colour of Hendrix – the blues filtered through the red-hot futurism of his electric guitar.

The tick-tock intro is made up of "tritones" which were considered so discordant and amusical to mediaeval ears that they were condemned as "the devil in music" and subsequently banned during the counter-Reformation. As the track grinds through the gears, however, it begins to defy gravity, halting only to highlight vocally one of psychedelia's most enduring phrases; "'Scuse me, while I kiss the sky", (or "this guy", as some revisionists heard it, hoping to find even more ambivalence in the lyric).

Confusion mounts, as does the song. There's a faint inkling of disappointment when the song threatens to be no more than another bout of chick trouble ("That girl put a spell on me"), though the idea that Hendrix could at least entertain the prospect of thralldom to a female represents an advance on the thinking of "Stone Free". Whatever, Hendrix is sucked further into the heavens as a series of solos ascend on the dying remains of their predecessors. Roger Mayer supplied Hendrix with the Octavia, in order to create the flute-like sounds emanating from Hendrix's guitar as it soars into the upper realms. Finally, still wondering where this trip's taking him, Hendrix is borne away into the fadeout, as if on a magic carpet of faintly oriental fretwork.

"Purple Haze" passes in and out like a dose of sulphur. Again, British audiences proved receptive to this strongest dose of Hendrix to date – the song reached no.3 and sold over 100,000 copies. In the US, where Warner/Reprise felt obliged to attach a sticker to the original tape box saying "Deliberate Distortion. Do Not Correct", for the benefit of its engineers, its fortunes were more mixed. The song was played hourly on the Los Angeles rock station KRLA, while bizarrely, the American comedian Bill Cosby approached Hendrix to play on an album he was recording, having written a new song to the melody of "Purple Haze" entitled "Hooray For The Salvation Army Band". For all this fuss, however, the single would stall at no. 65 in the American chart.

The subliminal suggestion of "Purple Haze", that the giddy ecstasy of 1967 was only the harbinger for an uncertain and dangerous future, would be proven accurate. The song's own future was rather rosier. It is among the most-loved and most covered of his songs, considered by many to be practically emblematic of the man.

51ST ANNIVERSARY

The b-side to "Purple Haze" epitomized the speed and sophistication of the *Are You Experienced* sessions. Though it contains five overdubs, linked together as if to form a single guitar line, it was recorded in a single day.

The multiple overdubs reflect the segmented feel of the song overall. It's another of Hendrix's morality tales concerning the perils of enforced domesticity, and goes through various phases. The first is an ostensible celebration of the institution of matrimony, taking for example the elderly couple who've been hitched for half a century and still have the hots for each other. But wait – that was the good side. Here comes the bad. Take another couple; ten years married with "a thousand kids", their mother a louse, the Dad "down the whiskey house". As if ignoring this demonstration of woe entirely, however, here's some clingy female flapping around Hendrix begging for him to lead her up the aisle, a clear symptom of her "weak little mind". Hendrix is having none of it and heads for the hills, showing his would-be spouse a clean pair of power chords.

The fears expressed in "51st Anniversary" are a constant in Hendrix's first few recordings – they're probably less evidence that he was in any imminent danger of any such commitment, perhaps more a sort of warning-stick with which to ward any of the numerous women he attracted who plotted to ensnare him. It was also a means of personalizing Hendrix's more abstract fear of containment of any kind, especially at a time when he was enjoying greater license for self-expression than he could previously have dreamt of.

While "51st Anniversary" isn't the most profound of Hendrix's lyrics, it's cleverer musically, particularly in the way the beat slows to a stealthy creep when the woman approaches with her marital proposal, and the flash of guitar speed as Hendrix scarpers from the prospect in horror.

THE WIND CRIES MARY

Hendrix's third single came as a shock to those who assumed he was a straight fire-and-feedback merchant. Not only does it show him to be capable of immense sensitivity, but also of a sweet melodic and lyrical turn of phrase. The song catches Hendrix in a subdued and repentant mood. No wonder – it was written following an argument with his London girlfriend Kathy Etchingham, prompted by remarks he'd made about what he regarded as her "terrible" cooking. A heated argument ensued, culminating in Etchingham hurling plates and pans about the kitchen of their flat before storming out to spend the night at the house of the Animals vocalist Eric Burdon.

While Hendrix was too proud to apologise, recalled Etchingham, he did present to her the lyric of this song. "Mary" was Etchingham's middle name. The line about "happiness staggering on down the street" and the broom sweeping up the broken pieces of yesterday's life clearly referred to her abrupt departure and the aftermath of broken crockery. Hendrix had managed to wreak from this almost comical dispute a honeyed, soulful hymn of penitence.

Kathy Etchingham, a hairdresser who already knew some pop stars including Keith Moon, was Hendrix's first girlfriend in Britain – they met the night he arrived in London in 1966, when Chandler asked her to walk Hendrix back to his hotel. No pliant dolly bird, she had a spirit to match her flowing red locks, and theirs was an often tempestuous relationship. In December 1966, they moved together into Ringo Starr's vacant flat in Montagu Square, scene of the now-legendary domestic dispute.

Etchingham reluctantly tolerated Hendrix's constant womanising, before she finally married Eric Clapton's chauffeur. Hendrix was devastated at her decision, but they remained lifelong friends. She held onto his record collection, and was eventually able to auction it off via Sotheby's in 1991 for £2,420. It now belongs to the Experience Music Project in Seattle.

True to non-monogamous form, it's emerged that Hendrix may actually have written the first draft for "The Wind Cries Mary" for a previous girlfriend – he always said it was "not about one or any person". One Mary Washington claimed she had seen the words "Somewhere a Queen is weeping/ Somewhere a King has no wife" in a poem Hendrix had written for her.

The lyric is strongly reminiscent of Bob Dylan, right down to the half-spoken cadences of the final verse. But there's a simplicity about Hendrix's home-brewed surrealism – "The traffic lights they turn blue tomorrow" – which is uniquely affecting.

Kathy Etchingham was Jimi's first lover on his arrival in London, and they would remain friends until his death.

39

HIGHWAY CHILE

When asked why it was that it took so long for Hendrix to be discovered, Lonnie Youngblood explained thus: "First of all, you got to remember he was a wanderer. Jimmy travelled light. Jimmy travelled with his guitar in a bag and his clothes in another bag. Jimmy wouldn't stay around." It's this restless spirit that accounts for his having slipped through so many fingers early on, a spirit that's celebrated in "Highway Chile" in which, in third person form, he sings about hitting the road, guitar swung across his back, longing to see the world and evade the discipline of his father, who deplored his pursuing a career as a musician.

Life on the road wasn't always as carefree as Hendrix has it sound on this rambunctious ditty. He was frequently disciplined, or sacked by martinet bandleaders, while late pay was often an issue too. "Guys would get fired in the middle of the highway because they were talking too loud on the bus or the leader owed them too much money," he told *Melody Maker* in 1969.

Although it offers further evidence of Hendrix's musical capabilities, "Highway Chile", b-side to "The Wind Cries Mary", fails to shine. Its opening guitar signature is horribly prescient of Deep Purple at their most weedily portentous, while the Chuck Berry-style progress of the verses only adds to the song's Jack-the-Laddish air. Again, Hendrix complains of a girl back home who did him wrong, a theme amply covered on "Hey Joe" and becoming just a little tedious by now.

FOXY LADY

The opening proper of the UK edition of *Are You Experienced* is pure sex music. Not sexual longing, not sexual conquest or braggadocio, just the sheer, velvet crush of sexual intercourse. One can only imagine the prurient mothers who feared for their daughters when they read about Hendrix in the *Daily Mirror*, gathering up their skirts in horror at this dirty salvo of carnal joy. The track's opening sends a tingle from deep in the loins up through the fretboard, as Hendrix enters, in a bass-heavy, testosterone blur of fuzztones and amplified static. The short, penetrative riff builds up, stroke by stroke, to a sense of climax; the guitar solo is a fluid and falsetto moan of sheer ecstasy.

There's a sense of Hendrix as a predator, making a raid on a henhouse – except, of course, the lady is a fox. She's just as up for it as Hendrix is.

When Hendrix growls, "Here I am, baby – I'm coming to git you!", you know and he knows that she's ready for him.

Perhaps "she" is Hendrix's guitar, Electric Lady, whose shrill, eloquent tones suggest how much she's enjoying his attentions. Most likely, "she" is an actual, or composite woman, though it was supposedly written as a tribute to Heather Taylor, later wife of Roger Daltrey.

With its dazed, no-frills riffology, "Foxy Lady" is a prototype for the later likes of Black Sabbath and some of the baser forms of heavy metal. But whereas heavy metal's sexual politics usually took the form of imaginary Viking conquests of one-dimensionally submissive females, the politics of "Foxy Lady" is spot on. This represents a lustful meeting of equals.

MANIC DEPRESSION

It's been suggested, most famously by American writer Nik Cohn, that Noel Redding and Mitch Mitchell, the rhythm section of the Experience were dispensable and, far from moaning about the royalties they received, should have been grateful to be paid anything at all.

This is widely accepted as harsh, indeed plain wrong. Redding's bass provided a solid underpinning for Hendrix, while Mitchell was more than capable of sustaining a frantic musical dialogue on equal terms with his guitarist. Nowhere is that better illustrated than on "Manic Depression".

Hendrix biographer David Henderson agrees that Redding and Mitchell played up a storm but makes the unsubstantiated suggestion that this was borne, on Mitchell's part out of a "strange contempt" for Hendrix. He also picked up on Redding's remark that he used to call Hendrix "a coon" ("and Jimi dug it!") as evidence that he resented playing second fiddle to Hendrix. Taken in context, Redding's comments are more indicative of crass taste and 1960s naïveté than true racism. Certainly, both Redding and Mitchell were deeply upset about Henderson's comments, unanimously refuted by those close to the Experience. What is for sure, however, is that both men had their pride. Redding had led his own band and played guitar himself, while Mitchell had a very solid musical pedigree. They would certainly have regarded playing with Hendrix as a challenge to be met, rather than shrunk from in cowering deference to his genius. Which was just what Hendrix needed.

The impetus for "Manic Depression" came after a dismal gig at the London Roundhouse that was capped by the theft of Hendrix's guitar. Chas Chandler remarked to Hendrix at a press reception that he was coming on like a "manic depressive". The song was recorded the following day.

With Hendrix doubling up on bass at key moments of emphasis, Redding plots a moody, aggressive line; he sounds real mean. Mitchell's dominant, octopus-on-speed percussion provides the "manic" element. Meanwhile, an overheated Hendrix grumbles amid the melee. He explained the key to the "frustrating mess" of "Manic Depression" when introducing the song on the *Live At Winterland* album. He said it was about the idea of being able to make love to his own music rather than the "same old everyday woman" – the sweet music that "drops from my fingers, fenders". His electric lady, his literal bedfellow in his paratrooper days, it seems, was the true love of his life, an impossible desire; his music, sweet music was untouchable. What he wanted was something his own music spoke

teasingly about, something better and more beautiful than sex. After all, once you've had your spurt of what the poet Rochester described as "all that Heaven allows", that's your little lot.

"Manic Depression" isn't borne out of an utter despondency but a chafing restlessness. Hendrix was too far ahead of the game, so out of sight that he must have felt invisible at times. It was depressing. The recalcitrant crowd at the Roundhouse hadn't got it; the squares who regarded him as something of a circus act, to step up and take a gander at, certainly didn't. Fortunately, Mitch Mitchell and Noel Redding *did* get it. As Redding acts as the anchorman on bass, Hendrix and Mitchell exchange a potent call-and-response series of lamentations before the song finally crashes and burns in a dark pool of feedback.

RED HOUSE

This was the first of many 12-bar blues that Hendrix would record. He may not even have recorded it had he not been cajoled to do so by producer Chas Chandler, who'd witnessed him mess about with a song Hendrix himself might have regarded as nothing special. He was steeped in the blues, from his days down South staying with relatives, and particularly since a meeting with fellow left-handed bluesman Albert King, who had made a great impression on the young Hendrix. But blue was just many of the colours on Hendrix's palate.

It was, however, traditional for the 1960s blues-boomers, from John Mayall to Jimmy Page, to lay down at least one blues track on their albums by way of homage. "Red House" was in accordance with that tradition, and properly observes the formalities. No studio trickery or avant-garde distortion here, although the opening blues yodel, the sort of opening gambit preferred by Robert Johnson on his 1930s recordings, almost sends the needle into the red before setting on down the well-trodden road of his musical ancestors.

The blues this may be, but in fact it's one of the most ebullient and playful numbers on the album. The lyric is a comic one – Hendrix, away from home "for about ninety-nine-and-one-half days" returns to pay a visit to his baby, only to find that she's changed the locks on the door. Never mind, Hendrix consoles himself. He still has his guitar, still has the open road and if his baby won't love him, here's the punchline – her sister will!

This could have been a throwaway number, a pastiche of the seeming restraints of the 12-bar form, except that Hendrix's dazzling fretboard phraseology, the casual eloquence of his playing and the effortless, almost thoughtlessly tossed-off way in which the notes tumble and cascade from his fingers is utterly unprecedented. It's a pure, awesome demonstration of Hendrix's supernatural talents. Other would-be bluesmen, black and white, sweated buckets to attain a fraction of the effects achieved here, which apparently cost Hendrix no more energy than it takes a cat to swish its tail.

"Red House" was excluded from the initial American release of *Are You Experienced*, for, as Hendrix related, unsure whether to laugh or cry: "They told me, Americans don't like blues, man!"

CAN YOU SEE ME

One of the very first songs to have been recorded in the *Are You Experienced* sessions, "Can You See Me" is, by the very high standards of the rest of the album, an undistinguished piece of bustling and blustering boogie. There are a couple of neat effects – a single electric twang that sounds like The Shadows' Hank Marvin being catapulted into outer space, and a deep bass arc that takes the song up to a warp factor of two. But Hendrix cuts a rather hollow and unattractive figure in the lyric.

Initially coming on like a schoolboy pouring scorn on the very idea that he's ever going to go begging and scraping to a woman who's left him – ha! Can you see me doing that? The very idea! – Hendrix ends up abandoning his position of feigned indifference and brusquely pleading with her, telling her she'd better come home like she's "supposed" to. The song ends with unnatural abruptness after barely two-and-a-half minutes, as if the musicians, despairing at the errant female Hendrix is trying to get through to, have downed tools in disgust. It also smacks of an exaggerated observation of the mid-1960s convention that album tracks be kept as short as possible.

LOVE OR CONFUSION

Originally intended as a single before Hendrix popped up with "Purple Haze", "Love Or Confusion" is caught in the throes of the same doubts as "Haze". Hendrix is unable to figure out whether the feelings he's caught up in are the natural urges of a true love or just some form of intoxication. Hendrix puts some distance between himself and the listener on this track by means of a Phil Spector-style echo device. It's as if he's some young

Cherokee brave, on the threshold of adulthood, who has gone up to a canyon ridge in order to survey the scene of his soul, be alone with his visions and call out to the gods for guidance. Is this the Real Thing, or did someone spike his drink again?

Roger Mayer's fuzz-pedal devices are really brought into their own on this track. With Mitch Mitchell's drumming swirling like a disorientating sky and Noel Redding's bass rumbling up as if from the caves way down below, the vast space in between is filled with an array of pyrotechnics dancing tantalisingly before Hendrix. Feedback drags like a Honda 750 caught in the mud, treble notes catch and refract the blinding sunlight, a whole range of tones and colours mingle and cohabit smokily down in the valley. The whole effect is one of hallucination and mind warp, psychedelic SFX the like of which proved to be a heady initiation to the audiences of the Sixties. Even tracks as radical as The Beatles' "Tomorrow Never Knows" hadn't been this vertiginous, hadn't stared this far down into the depths.

I DON'T LIVE TODAY

This song was, according to Hendrix, "dedicated to the American Indians and all minority depression groups", in which he included the militant Black Panthers. But most of the feeling in "I Don't Live Today" seems directed towards his Cherokee brethren, as signified by the pow-wow-style rhythmical opening.

Here, Hendrix laments the fate of the once-proud Native American Indian, dispossessed from the land with which his relationship was sacred, out of their time, vegetating on reservations, forced to eke out a living selling dream catchers to passing tourists. Speaking about their plight, Hendrix said, "It's just a really bad scene for them, you know. Like half of them are down in skid row, you know, drinking and completely out of their minds." Many in the emergent Black Power movement wished Hendrix would be as outspoken on the plight of African Americans but somehow, the displacement and ruin of Native Americans was closer to his heart.

The more the song broods, with its killer, downbeat riff and the throbbing, migraine effect of a hand-operated wah-wah, the more it seems to speak to the anguish of that minority depression group of one, Hendrix himself; "No sun comin' through my windows/ Feel like I'm living at the bottom of a grave." The first flat Hendrix occupied in London was above a pub in Soho, where he painted the entire place in black, even buying black

satin curtains, a sort of capsule of outer space in the middle of W1. While this was highly conducive to his cosmic imaginings, it can't have been a very cheering environment when his mood took a knock.

As Hendrix laments about "wasting your time away", his guitar ebbs away to nothing, before reactivating as Hendrix ups and embarks on a journey through hyperspace on a sonic time machine, hurtling through the dimensions like the penultimate sequence of *2001: A Space Odyssey*, occasionally moaning "there ain't no life nowhere". It's the first, strong stirring of his sci-fi futurist yearnings, a desire to break free from the small and constricted times he'd been born into.

MAY THIS BE LOVE

Far and away the prettiest track on *Are You Experienced*, "Waterfall" is a homage to Jimi's Cherokee guardian angel, the goddess of aquatic sanctuary. While Hendrix's relationship with earthbound females is often fraught and ultimately dissatisfied, he finds a higher form of bliss in a supernatural or spiritual idea of the "female", with whom he's quite happy about speaking of love. The opening, a descending shower of Hawaiian sliding chords, instantly transports us to this state of balm, as Mitchell's hovering drum patterns combine with Hendrix's beautiful, tropical meanderings to paint a picture of the sort of all-female aquatopia that Captain Kirk and his crew occasionally used to alight on in episodes of *Star Trek*.

The ideas sketched out here would be explored in much more depth on "1983... (A Merman I Should Turn To Be)". Here, the final descent of Hendrix's guitar into the lower registers hints at that oceanic solace to come. For now, this was simply another indication of Hendrix's versatility and his supreme lightness of touch.

FIRE

Given that fire is at the very core of Hendrix's artistic being, the ultimate metaphor for what he brought to rock music, it's something of a pity that the origins of this song should have been so prosaic. The story is a simple one. Hendrix was round at Noel Redding's mother's house, and feeling a bit cold. He asked Mrs. Redding if he could stand next to the fire. The phrase stuck with him, and he decided to build a bawdy song around it.

This is Hendrix back in a familiar earthbound mode, horny and hungry. A babe has caught his fancy. She doesn't care for Hendrix; she's already going steady. All the better, says Hendrix. He's just looking for a quickie, no romantic strings, all he wants is to unload his lust – or, as he puts it, in one of rock's more puzzling euphemisms, "let me stand next to your fire".

This is pretty straightforward stuff, almost a showcase for Mitch Mitchell's drumming which Hendrix doesn't bother to rise to challenge, his eyes fixed elsewhere. Mitchell and Redding join in on the chorus, like a couple of playground nerds egging on the school stud. But when Hendrix sings "Move over, Rover/And let Jimi take over," it's hard not to smile.

This is Hendrix the showman, the carnival sorcerer, bumping and grinding and waggling his tongue for the ladies. When he played at the London Astoria on the Engelbert Humperdinck tour, journalist Keith Altham suggested to Hendrix that he might want to liven up the song, and proceedings in general, by setting his guitar alight by way of a visual aid to "Fire". Hendrix agreed and some lighter fluid was sent out for. Onlookers were horrified, some believing Hendrix was trying to set fire to himself – in fact, like an inexperienced barbecue father, he'd accidentally applied too much fluid, sending flames shooting up several feet in the air, with Hendrix rocking back and blowing his hands. Once the audience realised it was theatre, they went into raptures – less so the Astoria manager, who threatened to sue for damages.

"Fire" was recorded on the same day the Experience discovered they'd reached no. 4 in the charts with their first single, "Hey Joe", which would account for its unbridled boisterousness.

THIRD STONE FROM THE SUN

With this extended piece, Hendrix seems to take a giant evolutionary stride before our eyes, with awesome consequences for humanity. Chas Chandler co-claimed responsibility for inspiring "Third Stone", saying that it is based on a story called *Earth Abides* by George R. Stewart. However, the scenario of the song, in which aliens visit earth, survey it and – finding no life form of worth except, for some reason, the "majestic hen" – decide to obliterate mankind, is all Hendrix's own.

"Third Stone" feels like an imaginary act of cosmic vengeance on the planet that was imprisoning his soul. Wheeling full-throttle through a deep space of drum and bass in a kinky machine of his own devising, Hendrix exchanges remarks with co-pilot Chas Chandler, who provides one half of the ultra-slow, Darth Vader-like opening dialogue. Initially, the main riff (later reprised by Cozy Powell on his 1974 hit "Dance With The Devil") is

pure tranquility bass. Wispy effects suggest dust or distant galaxies. But then, as the craft approaches the earth's atmosphere, turbulence hits, the booster engines roar, bits of the rocket fall away and Hendrix's guitar begins to judder. Finally, as Passover angel Hendrix delivers his harsh judgment, missiles are dispatched and, in a cataclysmic fretboard riot of collapsing skyscrapers and buckling metal, civilisation is destroyed.

Significantly, the last words with which Hendrix addresses the doomed planet are, "And you'll never hear surf music again". Here was the truth at the heart of this apocalyptic fantasy. Hendrix's rise to fame coincided with the end of American pop's glib sunshine years. Hendrix's arrival represented an eclipse of all that. As for Brian Wilson, the highly-strung genius behind the Beach Boys, it was as if he took Hendrix's words to heart. After 1966 Wilson went into exile, took to his bed and opted out of the remainder of the 1960s.

REMEMBER

Following the cosmic apocalypse, here is a gentle breather and an oddity in the Hendrix canon – an almost straight R&B number of clipped Stax-style soul reminiscent of Otis Redding. It's the only Hendrix track here that would have been obviously recognizable as within the tradition of mainstream black music. It's as if Hendrix is trying on one of his old session sidekick's tuxedoes for size, and experiencing a rare *frisson* of nostalgia.

Otis Redding and Jimi Hendrix both played the Monterey festival in 1967, and both went down huge. Hendrix represented the meteoric landing of rock's future, but Redding's magnificent set was a barnstorming reminder that a "trad" soul man like himself could more than hold his own among the burgeoning psychedelic set without having to don a kaftan. (Tragically, Redding died six months later in a plane crash). Similarly, once accepted on its own terms, "Remember" holds its own on *Are You Experienced*, with Hendrix rather sweetly calling for his lover to come back home, the mockingbird she bought him having fallen mute since the day she left.

It's a (slight) return for Hendrix to soul daze – but not a trip he'd be inclined much to repeat in the future.

ARE YOU EXPERIENCED

Based on a poem Hendrix wrote in late 1966 entitled "Trumpets And Violins, Violins", the title track of *Are You Experienced* is the album's best, one conceived and realized almost entirely in the studio. On its most basic, lewd and threatening level, it could be taken as a sexual initiation, with Hendrix aggressively propositioning a trembling virgin, mocking her for her nervousness as he prepares to deflower her.

Or, it could be drugs. The cakewalk shuffle of backwards guitar, drums and even bass, to the surreal accompaniment of Hendrix tolling out time on an out-of-tune piano, all add to the sense of a rite of passage into a bizarre world, a passage through the looking glass into a psychedelic beyond. For *Are You Experienced*, read, "have you dropped acid"?

Hendrix was "experienced" and, by way of proof, he embarks on a lengthy, backward guitar solo whose elaborateness is all the more remarkable in that Hendrix, playing forwards, simply harboured in his head an idea of how the solo should sound. It's spot on – a difficult and painful passage but no less exquisite for that.

Sex, drugs, maybe both – there's possibly a faint, unpleasant connotation of drug-induced date rape. But Hendrix admonished against taking this as just a simulated chemical rush: "Not necessarily stoned but beautiful". The initiation here is of rock'n'roll. "Are You Experienced" symbolises the altered state in which Hendrix left rock music, dragged through a hedge of electricity backwards, its horizons forcibly expanded. This was Experience indeed, perhaps the most intense in rock music to date.

AXIS: BOLD AS LOVE

Recorded	October 1966 – April 1967 at De Lane Lea, CBS & Olympic Studios.
Produced by	Chas Chandler.
Engineered by	Dave Siddle, Eddie Kramer and Mike Ross.
Musicians:	Jimi Hendrix (lead vocals, backing vocals, guitar, handclaps, piano), Noel Redding (bass, backing vocals), Mitch Mitchell (drums, tambourine, backing vocals, cowbell).

EXP

UP FROM THE SKIES

SPANISH CASTLE MAGIC

WAIT UNTIL TOMORROW

AIN'T NO TELLING

LITTLE WING

IF 6 WAS 9

YOU GOT ME FLOATIN'

CASTLES MADE OF SAND

SHE'S SO FINE

ONE RAINY WISH

LITTLE MISS LOVER

BOLD AS LOVE

In an age when bands and artists are practically urged to wait two or three years in between album releases, so as not to over-expose themselves, it seems extraordinary that no sooner had the Jimi Hendrix Experience completed their debut album than they headed straight back to Olympic Studios to commence work on the follow-up.

Again, there would be interruptions imposed by a heavy touring schedule. Worse, calamity struck when Hendrix misplaced the master tapes for the album's first side just before they were due to make the final mix, with no one having thought to make back-ups. In order to meet their deadline, the band were forced to go back to the studio and rework half the album, with the mixing now having to be completed in a single night.

Within a year of arriving in London, Hendrix had swiftly established his primacy in the rock world among his British-born guitar peers. There might have been an element of inverted racism in this worshipfulness in that the white blues rockers practically fetishised Hendrix's Realness, Blackness and Otherness, qualities they themselves couldn't attain. However, the notoriously unassuming and impeccably mannered Hendrix didn't crow at his newfound status but merely took advantage of the freedom it afforded him. Arrogance just wasn't part of his make-up.

There was, however, one incident involving Mick Jagger and his then-girlfriend Marianne Faithfull, in which he reverted to the predatory personality type he'd often exposed on *Are You Experienced*. Hendrix had bonded with Rolling Stones guitarist Brian Jones, although the latter was becoming marginalized from the group. Hendrix was aware that Jagger

The Rolling Stones. Relations were strained when Jimi tried to steal Mick Jagger's girlfriend, Marianne Faithfull.

Pete Townshend of The Who – like Hendrix, no great enthusiast for proper guitar maintenance.

was crowding Jones out of the band, which may have accounted for his behaviour at the Speakeasy, at a Hendrix gig attended by Jagger and Faithfull. Following an especially theatrical and emotion-drenched performance, the barrage of his own, groaning feedback a manifestation of his deadly build-up of raw sexuality, Hendrix came and sat himself between the couple. His back to Jagger, and his voice drowned out by the music from the PA, he propositioned Faithfull. She turned him down – but, years later, she was to confess that not having an affair with Jimi Hendrix was "the lasting regret of my life".

Having so swiftly conquered Britain, Hendrix made his first and telling assault on the USA at the 1967 Monterey International Pop Festival in California, a follow up to the famous "Human Be-in" which took place in San Francisco in the spring of that year. In many ways, this was the coming-out event for the late 1960s scene, not just for new acts like Jimi Hendrix and Laura Nyro but also for the emerging underground press who were given special privileges and access for the event. With Derek Taylor, press publicist for The Beatles, lending his organisational know-how to the festival, it managed not to collapse into the sort of unmitigated shambles in which hippie idealism usually resulted. All of the principal pop aristocracy lent their presence and profiles to the event, from the Beatles and the Stones to Smokey Robinson, all mellowed out in the spirit of love, unity, youth, international consciousness and some extremely potent Mexican marijuana.

Appearing in the blitzkrieg wake of the Who, following a heated discussion as to which band should go on first, The Experience took to the stage against the natural advantage of a huge, resplendent California sunset and delivered a set of such mounting, nuclear intensity it was as if their energy alone was responsible for dragging the sun down from the sky. They did cover versions – "Wild Thing" by The Troggs and Dylan's "Like A Rolling Stone" – familiar songs transmogrified into something hugely unfamiliar. By way of climax, Hendrix set fire to his guitar, kneeling over it religiously

The Monkees. Hendrix
supported them... it
seemed like a good
idea at the time.

and bidding the flames higher. As he quit the stage, the guitar lay there, continuing to burn, emitting a sustained electronic squeal, as if in its death throes. When the Who had smashed up their equipment it seemed petulant by comparison, like bratty delinquent Brit-boys trying to pass off their petty vandalism as modern art. When Hendrix destroyed his guitar, it seemed an altogether holier gesture, a ritual sacrifice, an act of purification. Everyone was in a state of sheer delirium at Hendrix's performance, with the exception of the hapless Grateful Dead, standing blinking in the wings, due to come on next, faced with the prospect of trying to follow him.

Hendrix should never have had to look back following Monterey. Yet only a couple of months later, he was victim again of the ridiculousness of 1960s pop promotion. He'd been booked by Mike Jeffery to go on tour with teeny-pop sensations the Monkees.

The Hendrix/ Monkees tour of 1967 has gone down in rock legend as one of the great mismatches of all time. Yet back then, it didn't appear to be such a terrible idea. The critical apparatus that would later come along and separate pop from "serious" rock hadn't yet been properly assembled, and the mass appeal of the Monkees alone led commentators to tout them as the "new Beatles". The Monkees' Mickey Dolenz and Peter Tork in particular certainly took themselves seriously, regarding themselves as peers, if not the equals of Hendrix. Tork even hung out with Jimi. As for Hendrix, there were still many on the scene who considered him (not least his own management) as much a showman as a musician. The Monkees tour, it was believed, would provide him with prime exposure.

Needless to say, however, the tour didn't work. To Hendrix's dismay, the young Monkees' teenybopper audience weren't ready for the rock bombshells the Experience threw at them in the opening act, yearning for the firecracker fizz and pop of their heroes, for whom they impatiently chanted during the support act's set. Hendrix finally gave in to his exasperation and flipped the finger at the audience. Looking for a way out of the tour, manager Chas Chandler put out a spoof press release written by critic Lillian Roxon, on the road with the band, stating that the right-wing group the Daughters Of The American Revolution had deemed Hendrix's stage act "too erotic" and "corrupting the morals of the American youth" and lobbied for Hendrix to be dropped from the tour. This nonsense was taken as gospel, reprinted faithfully in the press, including the *NME*, conveniently adding grist to Hendrix's "dangerous" image. If the Daughters Of The American Revolution were even aware that their name had been taken in vain, they kept quiet, perhaps themselves glad of the free publicity.

There, then, was Hendrix in mid-1967, having the greatest time of his life, having shown off the full breadth and volume of his potential in America, yet still hamstrung by the silliness of the 1960s pop machine to which, admittedly, he owed his breakthrough. *Axis: Bold As Love* reflects this "in-between" state. It's lighter, more diverse and sophisticated than *Are You Experienced* but with the exception of "If 6 Was 9", the songs all clock in at a very poppy three-minute average. The concept of the "Axis", as expounded on the title track, reflects what you might call Hendrix's apocalyptic idealism. The sleeve, however, which parodies Hindu iconography, showing the members of the Experience alongside Ganesh the elephant God, is a piece of period hippy-dippy bilge, for which Hendrix later disclaimed responsibility. There's overall a sense of Hendrix just beginning to spread his wings, but still as yet not having escaped his "plastic cage".

The album is also heavily influenced by Hendrix's increasing use of LSD, by now a rock commonplace. During the *Axis* sessions, Hendrix was taking the stuff on a daily basis, lending the resultant music a more liquid and airborne feel. Only "Spanish Castle Magic" retains the heaviness of *Are You Experienced*. There's greater emphasis, too, on Hendrix's abilities as a songwriter. Overshadowed as it is between the twin monuments of *Are You Experienced* and *Electric Ladyland*, *Axis: Bold As Love* has in the past been one of Hendrix's more neglected albums – by way of (over) compensation, many Hendrix aficionados have declared it to be his best work. That's overstating its merits – brilliant as it is, and as much fun as Hendrix and co are having here, you feel in his heart he's longing to do so much more.

EXP

POWERED BY
EARSPLITTING
FEEDBACK,
SWINGING IN
GREAT ARCS
FROM ONE
SPEAKER TO
ANOTHER

Following a short, mock-jingle twanged out by Hendrix, a radio pundit, played adeptly by former child actor Mitch Mitchell, introduces a "very peculiar-looking gentleman" who goes by the name of Mr. Paul Caruso. He's here to discuss the vexed question of whether or not such things as flying saucers exist. His voice tweaked to a helium falsetto to stress his nerdiness, the announcer invites him to scotch "this nonsense about spaceships and even space people."

In comes Mr. Caruso, a.k.a. Hendrix, his voice slowed to a stoned drawl, evidence of his supernatural heaviness of being. "As you all know, you just can't believe everything you see and hear. Now, if you'll excuse me, I must be on my way." Whereupon, to the gibbering of the announcer, "Mr Caruso" launches into the stratosphere, engines burning beneath him, powered by earsplitting feedback, swinging in great arcs from one speaker to another as he hurtles back and forth across the skies.

Evidence of the Experience's kooky sense of fun rather than of the existence of extra-terrestrials, "EXP" also functions as a scorching manifestation of Hendrix's electric horsepower, should he choose to wield it. "Paul Caruso" was the name of a harmonica player Hendrix befriended back in his days playing Greenwich Village. He would later crop up blowing his harmonica on "My Friend" on *First Rays Of The New Rising Sun*.

UP FROM THE SKIES

Those expecting Hendrix to come out with all guns blazing on his sophomore album would have been taken aback by "Up From The Skies". Skimming along to the languid brushstrokes of Mitch Mitchell, accompanied by the casually lucid chatter of wah-wah guitar, it's Hendrix at his most limber, even jazzy. Gil Evans, who orchestrated many of Miles Davis' works and in 1974 would make an orchestral album of Jimi Hendrix songs, counted this among his favourite songs. It's artless and sweatless – it's as if the guitar solo dribbles naturally and unconsciously from his fingers. But then, that's the mystery of swing, and swing is precisely what this delightful and too-brief number does.

The lyrics, however, provide a counterpoint. They're involved and inquisitive, with Hendrix adopting the persona of a traveller in space and time, looking down on earth from afar, dismayed that since his time away the planet has become out of kilter, ill-attuned with the universe – "I come back to find the stars misplaced". There's even a hint of the eco-consciousness that would only dawn properly on the world when photos of the planet were sent back from the moon in 1969. "Maybe it's just a change of climate . . ." ponders the traveller, whose last acquaintance with earth was during the ice age.

Hendrix is anxious to see if there is anything beyond the hippie dream other than platitudes like "Love the world" and hopeful that the new mother Earth, the Gaia-like sensibility he frequently hankered after in his songs, might prove genuinely to offer hope for the restoration of mankind.

The self-deflating pay-off line in the fadeout is delivered with a chuckle: "Aw, shucks – if my Daddy could see me now." Although an entertainer himself, Hendrix Sr. had deplored the idea of his son going into the music business, and when Jimi rang him to announce his arrival in London, his father hung up in disgust, not least because the charges were reversed. Now Hendrix was riding the cosmos, and it didn't take long for the old man to come around.

SPANISH CASTLE MAGIC

Anyone concerned, following "Up From The Skies", that they were in for an album of psychedelic cocktail party jazz was swiftly appeased by "Spanish Castle Magic", a heavy-duty rocker pushed well up the running order so as to reassure traditional Hendrix listeners. A favourite of the headbanger's wing of the Hendrix Appreciation Society, it's a devastating onslaught of serrated tonnage with multi-dubbed guitars stampeding at you like a cavalry, kicking up an electric dust storm.

If there was a tiny doubt as to whether "Are You Experienced" was, in fact, a song about initiation into the world of drugs by an experienced tour operator, there's little here. "No, it's not in Spain," says Hendrix, as if the dumb chick he's trying to induce hasn't quite caught his meaning. As with "Are You Experienced", the sheer immersion in the sound represents a sort of unholy baptism. Allusions to "cotton candy" are to be well understood, while any worries about harmful side-effects are played down by the acid tutor; "Just a little bit of a daydream here and there." The "just float your little mind around" line sounds, for all the world, like "just fucked your little mind around", and you wonder if this is as "accidental" as the big teaser/prick-teaser lyrical confusion on The Beatles' "Day Tripper".

In fact, by the standards of the day and not least his rock'n'roll peers, Hendrix was not an immoderate consumer of narcotics. The trouble was, most of his fans and hangers-on assumed from songs like "Spanish Castle Magic" that he preferred to be as high as a kite at all times, and obliged him by spiking his drinks while his back was turned.

WAIT TILL TOMORROW

Unfortunately, "Wait Till Tomorrow", probably the most disposable number on *Axis* . . . doesn't maintain the momentum of "Spanish Castle Magic". It's a vaudevillian throwback to Hendrix's R&B days, the story of an elopement gone disastrously wrong. There stands Hendrix, ladder against the wall, desperately trying to persuade "Dolly Mae" to climb out of her window and join him, only she's got cold feet. Noel Redding provides the shrill, falsetto chorus for the cartoonishly prim Dolly Mae ("I think we'd better wait till tomorrow"). But tomorrow's too late – a silhouette appears and there's Dolly's Daddy, shooting Jimi dead where he stands, the words

"wait till tomorrow" echoing ironically in his ears as he expires.

Musically, "Wait Until Tomorrow" isn't up to much, until Mitch Mitchell decides to enliven matters with an explosive volley of bebop percussion just before the outtro. This is a comedy number, certainly capturing the exuberant mood of the musicians in the studio and, some would argue, an antidote to the heavy bouts of self-indulgence to which the Experience were prone. However comedy and music, like ice cream and gravy, rarely mix well, and joke numbers like this are often the worst form of self-indulgence among musicians.

AIN'T NO TELLING

Originally scribbled on the stationery of the Hyde Park Towers hotel, where Hendrix stayed on first arriving in London, "Ain't No Telling" is one of the earliest songs he penned on coming to England. It was based around Hendrix's homespun formula for men experiencing relationship difficulties. "1. Don't answer the phone 'cause it might be your baby. 2. Don't act the fool when she arrives. 3. After breakfast, look at your watch and say 'It's time to pack'."

A straight-ahead number in the "Stone Free" vein, "Ain't No Telling" is modern blues with an outboard rock motor and psychedelic wings attached – not least in the couplet "Oh Cleopatra she's driving me insane/ she's trying to put my body in her brain." Hendrix is upping sticks like the itinerant bluesman he is at heart, unable to make any promise about when he's going to be coming back. He does at least sound sincere when he says he hopes it'll be tomorrow, but this is belied by the song's best moment, a sonic effect that suggest he isn't just hitting the road, he's disappearing into another dimension, leaving only a trail of metallic echo in his wake.

LITTLE WING

Just 2 minutes 24 seconds long, "Little Wing" is one of the most precious, if evanescent moments in Hendrix's entire catalogue. It was popularised by Stevie Ray Vaughan in the 1980s, though covering this song, indeed any Hendrix song, was always liable to be an invidious task.

Conceived as Hendrix stared out over the fairground at the Monterey Festival, basking in a moment of reflective solitude at his success there, it's a hymn of praise to his (Native American) muse, based on what he described as a "very, very simple Red Indian style". Hendrix's many girlfriends might each have liked to have thought they were the model for the song but it speaks of a feminised, supernatural spirit to whom no earthly woman, with the possible exception of his late mother (that's to say, his dim memory of her) could measure up.

The character of Little Wing visits on Hendrix rare moments of sublime tranquility and consolation, as well as inspiration, her "circus mind that's running wild" and "moonbeams and fairytales" providing the stuff of Hendrix's imaginative landscape. She represents a state of grace that's beyond flesh, beyond sex, in the face of which even Hendrix's machismo melts. Hendrix paid further homage to her on "One Rainy Wish" and also "Angel".

Emerging like a butterfly from its chrysalis, the song drips with an almost melancholic sense of rapture, the guitar solo rising like cream, the fairy bell notes of glockenspiel falling like teardrops. If there's an underlying sense of sadness to the song, it's because Little Wing's visits are so sporadic and, like this track itself, too brief. Several more verses of this would have been more than tolerable.

IF 6 WAS 9

This was one of the tracks on the master tapes that Hendrix mislaid, and the one the band, Chas Chandler and engineer Eddie Kramer had the most difficulty in recreating. Following one unsuccessful take after another, Noel Redding recalled that he had a tape containing a very rough, early mix of the track back at his flat. He was sent off to fetch it by cab, but it turned out to be so wrinkled it had to be ironed in order to be usable in the studio. Only then were they able to recall how they'd originally achieved its effects.

At 5 minutes 32 seconds, "If 6 Was 9" feels like an odyssey compared to the rest of the album. The erotic choice of numerals is probably deliberate – "If 3 Was 7" really wouldn't have sounded quite right. But there's nothing really coy going on here. This is Hendrix exhibiting his dark side, his spoken voice emerging from a deep void, extolling a defiant fatalism that is all the more disturbing when you consider his actual fate. "I'm the one that's gonna have to die when it's time for me to die," he drawls into the mic, chewing gum in the ice-cool, laissez-faire spirit of the song. According to those who knew him, Hendrix, while he enjoyed life, never expected to live that long – or, perhaps, like the Who, couldn't really conceive of growing old.

"If 6 Was 9" works at two lyrical levels and at two different paces. The bass quickens as Jimi sneers at a "white collar conservative" in the street, viewing him with barely concealed loathing. But Hendrix is determined to "wave my freak flag high", one of his key additions to the hippie lexicon. All of which amounts to so much "square"-bashing, a now-hackneyed sentiment, particularly in this post-punk, post-modern era.

It's when Hendrix falls in with the lengthy intervals of Mitch Mitchell's beat that the song is much more interesting. Let the sun refuse to shine, let the mountains fall into the sea, Hendrix don't mind. Let the hippies cut off their hair, Hendrix doesn't care. His absolute self-assurance is transcendental. "Let it be – it ain't me." Once again, Hendrix imagines himself as not really of this planet, his true spiritual essence residing outside of and beyond the earth, beyond harm. And so, as his guitar intimates of cataclysms yet to come, Hendrix remains oblivious, engaging in shrill blasts of whale song from the Olympian heights of the upper registers. And, when you contemplate Hendrix's posthumous fate, his music still shrieking and reverberating down the ages, more "alive" in many respects than when he was still around and only dimly recognised for what he was, you could argue that with "If 6 Was 9", he got it just about right.

YOU GOT ME FLOATIN'

Although never released as a single, "You Got Me Floatin'" is the poppermost track on the album. With Hendrix and Mitch Mitchell chopping out a metronomic, pop/funky rhythm in tandem, it's infectious and simple, swinging like Carnaby Street. Whereas "Purple Haze" is riven with doubt and ambiguity, this no-nonsense track is clearly an upper. Ostensibly, it's a paean to a woman whose very presence sends him into a tizzy of infatuation, albeit one that's not likely to last long, a boyish infatuation that, as night falls, becomes something rather more mannish; "that's when my desires start to show."

It's at this point that the song takes on a sleazy, X-rated quality, with an erotic squirm of backward guitar. Conversely, the song could be taken as a coded hymn to the merits of certain chemical substances, the backward taping being the effect of the hallucinogens kicking in (although Hendrix inserts the word "naturally" in order to cover his tracks), leaving innocent pop pickers who'd clambered aboard this pop carousel stumbling off, rather green in the face.

There's no harm in taking the song either way, as was doubtless the intention. It's certainly one of Hendrix's more accessible numbers, which deserves wider renown, maybe even a posthumous, long-overdue re-release as a single. The way the rhythm crashes back in to disrupt the reverie of the second backward solo is one of those Hendrix moments which snap your head right back.

CASTLES MADE OF SAND

A showcase for Hendrix's developing skills as a lyrical storyteller, "Castles Made Of Sand" is a psychedelia-tinted parable, featuring three scenarios. The first features a drunken man thrown out of the house by his wife, their once-happy marriage now a broken shambles, a pitiful spectacle for the neighbours to "gossip and drool" over. The second features a young Indian brave, who since the age of ten has dreamt of becoming a warrior chief. He grows up and here he is on the eve of battle, looking forward to his initiation and "singing his first war song". Unfortunately, the enemy makes a surprise attack during the night and kills him in his sleep.

Finally, a young girl, mute, disabled and thoroughly miserable with her lot, decides to take her own life by drowning herself in the sea. However,

THE SONG TAKES
ON A SLEAZY,
X-RATED QUALITY,
WITH AN EROTIC
SQUIRM OF
BACKWARD
GUITAR

just as she draws up to the shore, the sight of a "passing golden wing ship" miraculously restores her ability to walk and talk.

Jimi's brother Leon had his own interpretation of the song. "It's about my family. The Indian war chief is about me. The first verse is about mom and dad fighting, and the third verse is about my mom and her dying."

A modern take on Robert Burns' line about the best laid plans of mice and men, "Castles Made Of Sand" is beautifully illustrated by an elaborate criss-cross of backward guitars which denote the perverse tide of fate, which has a way of undoing all of mankind's built-up expectations, though not always for the worse. The scenario about the Indian brave would have had particular resonance in an era when young men were being sent to Vietnam, only to be scythed down before they even had a chance to discover what it was all about. However, in 1967, ex-paratrooper Hendrix was still for the war. Perhaps this was a case of the artist's imagination running ahead of his intellect.

SHE'S SO FINE

Noel Redding takes the lead vocal on his own "She's So Fine", a paean to a mysterious sunshine hippie chick who is the object of his priapic longings. Effervescent and awestruck, it bears some resemblance to the Who's "I Can See For Miles". Hendrix chimes in on backing vocals, as well as an extended wolf-whistle of a guitar solo.

ONE RAINY WISH

Based in part on "My Diary", a song he'd written with Rosa Lee Brooks, a singer he met on the road in late 1963, "One Rainy Wish" is another Arcadian revisiting of Hendrix's muse. This time, she appears to him via a dream, most probably of the wet variety. Hendrix finds himself in some sort of magical forest, underneath a star-filled sky of eleven moons, flanked by sun-kissed blue mountains. There she waits for him, beneath a tree, toying with a flower. The moment she sets eyes on him, she steals his heart and Hendrix wakes up.

The opening of "One Rainy Wish" is an exquisite, myriad guitar description of the soft-focus hues of gold, rose, misty blue and lilac in which the dream is bathed. But then, unexpectedly, the song gives way to harsher, heavy metal earth tones as Hendrix's vocals intensify to a hoarse scream. It's as if his loins are seething with frustration that he can't somehow break into his own memory bank and make his way back to that forest, meet again the recumbent, magical female who took possession of his heart. It's driving him crazy. All he can do is recount the maddeningly beautiful dream to anyone who cares to listen, recreate it in electric watercolours.

LITTLE MISS LOVER

An aggressive, teasing come-on in the tradition of "Foxy Lady", "Little Miss Lover" is Hendrix at his absolute down-and-dirtiest, meanest and funkiest. It's a touchstone for the badass superfly funk of Curtis Mayfield and Funkadelic in the 1970s, as well as the ubiquitous funk-metal of the likes of Living Colour and Red Hot Chili Peppers in the 1980s and 1990s. Even the "punk-funk" of UK groups like Gang Of Four and 23 Skidoo is full of echoes of "Little Miss Lover".

Swiftly recovered from the aching wistfulness of "One Rainy Wish", Hendrix is in easy, cocksure mode here: "Well, I really don't need any help little girl/But I believe you could help me out anyway." He even breaks off, quite unnecessarily you would have thought, to consult the "gypsy in me" to check that the strangely stirring feeling he is experiencing is lust for Miss Lover, and, having received final confirmation, goes ahead with his play. It's all pretty knockabout jive, with the testosterone level boosted by Mitchell and Redding's leery cheer-a-longs.

Hendrix's chat-up lines may be resistible but his guitar lines aren't. Never has his wah-wah sounded so lascivious and tumescent as here. Mitchell and (especially) Redding cook up a rhythmical stew of bump'n'grind, and the sheer overall cut and thrust of "Little Miss Lover" is enough to steam up the windows and make the horses restless.

BOLD AS LOVE

The album's title, keynote track is based on Hendrix's quasi-mystical obsession with the axis of the earth, one that he had felt most keenly when aboard an airplane, thousands of feet above the clouds, staring back down at the planet. The "axis" is an integral concept in Eastern religions – in the whirling dervishes, for instance, who spin on their axis in order to become vessels for the energy of God. Hendrix was fascinated by the notion of the earth's axis as the central source of all power, the vital link between heaven and earth. It was the source of the electromagnetic energy that fed his own music; even the spinning of a record on a turntable reminded him of the power of the axis.

Tilt the axis, reasoned Hendrix, and the whole world would be turned inside out, upside down, with the oceans being displaced and vast new continents created. Hendrix imagined the condition of falling in love as being similar to this sort of seismic alteration. As he made his transatlantic flights, first from New York to London in 1966 and then from London to Monterey in 1967, he felt the earth was tilting fatefully in his favour, that the axis was blessing his endeavours.

Hendrix invokes the axis on "Bold As Love", which commences with the word "anger" and a bellicose chord that strikes a jolting note of aggression. But it soon develops into one of Hendrix's most sensitive and soul-searching ballads, the tingling of his guitar adding to the sense of a romantic serenade, rose between teeth, gypsy heart flaming. Lyrically, it's a display of the many different colours that make up the various aspects of his character.

Purple and green are the nastier moods that stalk his soul, a king and queen who represent aggression and envy. Ranged against them, thankfully, are the "life-giving waters" of blue, and an entire army of turquoise so benign they have difficulty grasping the idea of conflict. Then there's proud, confident red with his "trophies of war" and "ribbons of euphoria", which represent Hendrix's creative and perhaps sexual potency. However, there's also orange, the part of Hendrix that is willing but inexperienced, and yellow, which, Jimi admits with reference to the Donovan song, is "not so mellow" but signifies a streak of cowardice.

It's this colour that is giving Hendrix cold feet as he hesitates to commit himself completely and wholeheartedly to the object of his tentative love. In order for him to be worthy of "a rainbow like you" he must, like her, similarly reconcile all of the diverse elements of his character, making peace with himself, banishing his fears, be "bold as love" and become nothing less than a serene whole. Only the all-knowing axis can help him create such unity from diversity.

This seems like the final note of the song as it fades away. But then, following a drum fanfare from Mitchell, it rears up again, duly emboldened, and Jimi undertakes a wailing guitar dervish of his own, speaker-to-speaker phasing adding to the sense of the axis in full rotation. Phasing was first used on 1959's "The Big Hurt" by Miss Toni Fisher, and later by the Small Faces on "Itchycoo Park". But, as ever, Hendrix elevated a pre-existing technology from a gimmicky feature on a record to a starring role.

It's the perfect climax to the album, demonstrating Hendrix's rainbow diversity both as a musician and as a human being, and he pulls out all the stops and pours all his myriad energies into this aurally dizzying outtro.

ELECTRIC LADYLAND

Recorded	October 1966 – April 1967 at De Lane Lea, CBS & Olympic Studios.
Produced by	Chas Chandler.
Engineered by	Dave Siddle, Eddie Kramer and Mike Ross.
Musicians:	Jimi Hendrix (lead vocals, backing vocals, guitar, handclaps, piano), Noel Redding (bass, backing vocals), Mitch Mitchell (drums, tambourine, backing vocals, cowbell).

. . . AND THE GODS MADE LOVE

HAVE YOU EVER BEEN (TO ELECTRIC LADYLAND)

CROSSTOWN TRAFFIC

VOODOO CHILE

LITTLE MISS STRANGE

LONG HOT SUMMER NIGHT

COME ON (LET THE GOOD TIMES ROLL)

GYPSY EYES

BURNING OF THE MIDNIGHT LAMP

RAINY DAY, DREAM AWAY

1983. . . (A MERMAN I SHOULD TURN TO BE)/

MOON, TURN THE TIDES ... GENTLY, GENTLY AWAY

STILL RAINING, STILL DREAMING

HOUSE BURNING DOWN

ALL ALONG THE WATCHTOWER

VOODOO CHILD (SLIGHT RETURN)

When Jimi Hendrix entered New York's Record Plant in mid-April 1968 to work on the third and, as it turned out, final album by the Jimi Hendrix Experience, he did so in truly turbulent times. Personally, professionally, musically and historically, things were working up to a head.

On April 4, 1968, Martin Luther King had been assassinated, sending American cities into violent convulsions. Later that year, Bobby Kennedy too was assassinated. Yet while America was being torn apart by riots, as the blowback from the conflagration in Vietnam came in the form of demonstrations and stand-offs with the authorities, Hendrix's dominant mood was one of euphoria. Anyone who knew him in that period remembers him with a hat tilted on his head and a smile permanently attached to his face. He was having a ball. Too much of a ball for some.

The Experience had started laying down basic tracks for *Electric Ladyland* in Olympic Studios in Barnes, though, in fact, recording had begun before work on *Axis: Bold As Love* was completed. There was an inclusive air about the sessions. Brian Jones had even dropped by, attempting to add a piano track to "All Along The Watchtower" which, unfortunately, had to be ditched, owing to his zonked condition.

Then, at the behest of their ever-exacting co-manager Mike Jeffery, the Experience were whisked over to America to undertake a frantic, criss-cross

Martin Luther King Jnr – his death in April 1968 inspired one of Jimi's most emotional (albeit unrecorded) performances.

tour of America, the schedule of which barely allowed them time to visit the bathroom. With very little thought given to geographical convenience, the tour would prove disruptive to the recording of the double album. Hendrix made his base in New York, block-booking studio time at the Record Plant, which benefited not only from state-of-the-art facilities but also from its proximity to clubs like The Scene and Ungano's, where Hendrix would hang out in lengthy after-hours jam sessions with rock peers like Eric Clapton and Jeff Beck.

Although not a native New Yorker, Hendrix felt that this was a triumphant homecoming, his "lap of honour" as Chas Chandler put it. Barely two years earlier, having just dropped off the chitlin' circuit, he had been an obscure young black musician scratching around for a foothold on the local club scene in that most cold-shouldered of towns. Now he was back, and New York was at his disposal. He enjoyed the jam sessions because he felt vindicated in the company of fellow, virtuoso musicians whose respect he craved. Hendrix was always a little embarrassed by his lack of formal tuition and inability to read music. Although it's clear his inflammatory, intuitive genius left most of his relatively tepid fretboard muso contemporaries trailing in his wake, a small part of him still blushed a little at the derision of those who dismissed him as a pop freak, a gimmick merchant. The jam sessions would spill over into the making of the album, as would numerous, extraneous hangers-on who would pile into the Record

Chandler with Hendrix. He quit as producer during the sessions for Electric Ladyland, Hendrix's greatest album.

ELECTRIC LADYLAND IS THE SOUND OF THE EXPERIENCE ON FIRE

Plant, with Hendrix too gratified at their adulation to exclude them.

This latter nuisance would prompt Chas Chandler to make his break from Hendrix. He looked on with dismay at the studio time wasted by the groupies. He despaired at the number of re-takes and remixes of tracks like "Gypsy Eyes". When he was in the Animals they'd recorded "House Of The Rising Sun" in a single take and still had change from twenty bucks. He deplored the unraveling of the tight three-piece he'd help conceive and the demise of the three-minute bundles of pop/rock/funk/psychedelia which had slingshot them to fame. The Record Plant was becoming the house of the rising self-indulgence. "There were a lot of hangers-on turning up at the studio and any artist in that situation is going to end up playing to the gallery instead of to the tape machine," he said. Feeling he was no longer being listened to, Chandler resigned as producer during the making of *Electric Ladyland*, eventually selling his share of the management to Mike Jeffery for $300,000 cash and future considerations.

He was right to do so. For, while some of his misgivings were valid, he had taken Hendrix as far as he was able. He'd been shrewd in whisking Hendrix off to London to make that his launch pad, but that done, so was Chandler's work. Hendrix was too large a spirit for the fickle confines of Carnaby Street. He'd done pop. Now he was heading west.

Sure, he was having a ball but this wasn't the sort of career-destroying bacchanalia of Sly Stone's *There's A Riot Goin' On* sessions. He wasn't just partying when he jammed; he wasn't just vacillating when he insisted on all those re-takes. Hendrix was looking to broaden his sonic palate. This was serious. This was the future.

Hendrix had been annoyed in the past that the musical visions in his head had often been botched due to lack of time or lack of care on the part of those responsible in the studio. This time, he said, "[the album] wasn't just slopped together. Every little thing on there means something." The key to *Electric Ladyland* would be his collaborative work with sound engineer Eddie Kramer, who helped to realise what Hendrix described as "3D sounds"; lightning and futuristic feats of electronic wizardry on tracks like "House Burning Down". Furthermore, through his jamming connections, Hendrix was aware that in 1968, a new cross-pollination was blowing in the air, especially in New York. Miles Davis was on the point of sending shockwaves through jazz with *In A Silent Way* and *Bitches Brew*, with his use of electric instruments. Some saw this as populist crudity, cynical mongrel breeding with rock elements. Others applauded Davis for at last expanding the jazz lexicon, which even at its most avant-garde had, with the extreme exception

of Sun Ra, proven strangely resistant to electronics. Davis was embracing rock just as Hendrix was embracing jazz. They'd mingle in similar space.

Noel Redding was also a victim of Hendrix's new expansiveness. As well as being understandably peeved to turn up to the studio to find nobody there, or the place full of strangers and his seat taken, Redding was becoming marginalised in the music-making process. Hendrix's new, hands-on approach extended to playing the bass himself, or roping in outsiders like Jack Cassady, or, on "Still Raining, Still Dreaming", not bothering with bass guitar at all. Drummer Mitch Mitchell was more tenacious and amenable (though had Hendrix been a dab-hand at the sticks, it might have been a different story). The disaffection of Redding, however, would eventually mean the end of the Experience. They finally disbanded in 1969. Redding was cut out of Hendrix's future plans, though the bassist had to find this out from a newspaper reporter.

Electric Ladyland was, undoubtedly a rock album, albeit rock on the point of evolving into something else. The title was Hendrix's own pet name for his guitar. At Monterey, Hendrix had set his guitar alight onstage in what one writer had described as a symbolic act of Dadaist destruction. *Electric Ladyland* is the sound of The Experience on fire, yet at the same time going up in flames.

Buddy Miles felt he was paying the album the ultimate compliment in saying it was "up there with *Sergeant Pepper*" yet besides *Electric Ladyland*, *Pepper* sounds like a small, period piece of psychedelic whimsy. *Electric Ladyland* is perhaps the most incandescent, if not the greatest rock album ever made. Its sheer range of moods is mountainous. It embodies all of the dark and light energy of 1968 – the year the 1960s peaked in intensity.

Jimi Hendrix in the studio. More than with previous albums, on Electric Ladyland Hendrix would use the recording studio and its mixing desk almost as musical instruments in their own right.

There were complaints about the costs of the album (which "soared" to $60,000), the length of time it took to make (almost a year!) and the excess of studio fiddling (it was recorded on 8 and 12-track). True, some time was wasted. Hendrix casually invited a cab driver that dropped him off at the studio to come jam with him. The cabbie took him at his word, turning up 30 minutes later. He and Hendrix jammed for six hours, Jimi lacking the heart to kick the poor guy out. Yet all of these quibbles are laughably ironic in the twenty-first century.

There were complaints, too, about the cover sleeve of the album's British release, conceived by Kit Lambert, who hadn't quite gotten with the new programme. It featured a score or so of naked young women who were paid £5 each to remove their tops (and a further £3, according to the photographer David Montgomery, to remove their underwear). What might have seemed a with-it act of provocation in swinging 1960s sexist Britain now looks lame and misconceived. Thanks to the sleeve, the album was banned in various UK towns. A Mr Hugh Robertson, a record shop owner in York objected; "There is no need for sleeves like this." Hendrix, oddly enough, agreed. He hadn't been consulted about the cover, he didn't think it flattered the women, and spoke out against it.

Praise for the album was, in some quarters, faint, with many critics feeling that Hendrix had over-reached himself. Frank Kofsky, writing for *Jazz & Pop*, sniffed that he didn't think it was "absolutely essential that we be given a long and sometimes monotonous double album to digest" while conceding that the album was an "overall solid achievement". Another review breathlessly declared that the album was a "shattering" one that "rivets you to the spot". John Landau concluded that "Hendrix was "tops" and 1968 was his year. However, even among those contemporary enthusiasts, there's a feeling that they didn't know just what had dropped into their hands, hot from the skies. Rock's critical language certainly hadn't developed to the extent that Hendrix had, while Hendrix had far exceeded public expectations of him as the mere "wild man of rock".

Electric Ladyland eventually reached no. 1 in the States and no. 5 in Britain, but Hendrix remained dissatisfied that the colours and sounds of the album still hadn't matched the colours and sounds in his own head. "We really got about half of what we wanted to say in it," he said, promising that the next album would be exactly as he wished. Given that this was the last fully realised studio recording Hendrix made in his lifetime, we can only dream of how he might have gone about exceeding this, his crowning achievement.

. . . AND THE GODS
MADE LOVE

Recorded the day after he had played a benefit for the Martin Luther King
Memorial Fund, Hendrix winced in advance at the flak that he seriously
expected for this audacious 81-second instrumental intro. "We're putting it
right at the beginning, to get it over with," he explained to the *Melody
Maker* writer Alan Walsh. Beginning with what sounds like the distant
reverberations of a cosmic bouncing bomb, a track of Hendrix saying, "OK,
one more time" is reversed and slowed down to a stentorian, alien drone.
Then there is a drenching spray of feedback, before this "sound painting"
judders and recedes.

The track could be taken as its word – a sonic transcription of a deity in the throes of ejaculation, a copious burst of electronic jism, divinely fertile. Or you could take it as a manifesto for the record to come, a pure sample of the new musical ether in which the album is suspended. Certainly, it's a stunning and, in rock music, an unprecedented piece of liquid sculpture. Originally entitled "At Last The Beginning" it leaves you in no doubt that what is to come will be an experience that not even the Experience have prepared you for.

HAVE YOU EVER BEEN (TO ELECTRIC LADYLAND)

Based on musical sketches made during the sessions for *Axis: Bold As Love* and in the same romantic spirit as "Little Wing", "Have You Ever Been (To Electric Ladyland)" is Hendrix at his most crushingly sweet. His creamy, falsetto vocals are reminiscent of the Impressions' Curtis Mayfield and Ronnie Isley of the Isley Brothers, both of whom would influence Hendrix (who played with the Isleys), both of whom he would posthumously influence in turn when Mayfield and the Isleys redefined themselves in the 1970s. It was on the nectar of tracks like this that they would draw. As for Hendrix himself, who never really believed in his own voice and was always urging Chas Chandler to bury it further in the mix, he was astonished at the beauty fluttering out of his own mouth. "I can sing! I can sing!" he reportedly broke off to yell, during recording.

After three, backwardly taped beats, Hendrix invites us aboard the magic carpet to the otherworldly splendours of Electric Ladyland, where sounds, motion and emotion disport as part of one liquid whole. Urging us to "cast all of your hang ups over the side (he slips what could be a "sui" on the echo just before the "side) he bids us contemplate the "love filled sea" which vaguely merges into a yonder "loveland" where good and evil lay side by side as electric love penetrates the sky. It's a notion of blissfulness based on absolute self-loss and the unity, better even than sexual, of all things. All of which, in the wrong hands, could sound like the most insubstantial of drug-induced, theologically dubious fantasy. However, in Hendrix's infinitely capable hands, weaving silvery, silken riffs, creating weightless studio effects and trailing away on a cirrus trail of guitars, the fantastic notion seems as palpable as ectoplasm.

CROSSTOWN TRAFFIC

In stark contrast, Hendrix eschews his angelic garb for scuffed leather on "Crosstown Traffic" which is Hendrix at his most boogie-driven dirty and street-bound. In 1990, the track was featured in a television advert for Wranglers, and it's the Hendrix many people feel most comfortable with – fast and raunchy. One of the tracks Chas Chandler had a strong early hand in producing at Olympic studios, it was certainly a song Hendrix's management felt comfortable with. It was released as a single in November 1968, virtually in tandem with the album, to Hendrix's chagrin. He complained that it came "from a different set . . . they always take out the wrong ones".

Although hardly typical of *Ladyland*, "Crosstown Traffic" is a sinful pleasure. Its choppy, funky riff is reminiscent of the sort of stuff he used to grind out on the chitlin' circuit. The track is redolent of Manhattan – you sense the onrush of Buicks, the steam rising from the drains, that sweet, strangely toxic smell that tells you you're in New York. All of this, topped off with a guitar solo accompanied by Hendrix emitting kazoo-like blasts achieved by means of a comb and cellophane.

THE FINEST VOODOO ALBUM THAT ANY ROCK GROUP HAS PRODUCED

Whereas on the likes of "...Ladyland", womankind is represented as a state of grace, here, she's just a cheap, fun-loving tramp along for a ride. One groans a little as Hendrix pursues the car/sex metaphor all the way down the fast lane: "Ninety miles an hour, girl/Is the speed I drive" . . . "I'm not the only soul accused of hit and run/Tyre tracks all across your back/I can see you had your fun!" It's Hendrix at his most naughty, yet still, in its rude velocity, touched with genius.

VOODOO CHILE

When *Rolling Stone* reviewed *Axis: Bold As Love*, they described it as "the finest voodoo album that any rock group has produced". Taken with this description, Hendrix instantly decided to re-name "Catfish Blues", a track he was working on. Hereafter, it was "Voodoo Chile".

Somewhat hard-to-verify claims have been made concerning Jimi Hendrix's true involvement with the world of voodoo. One Eddie Kirkland, who played with John Lee Hooker, famously asserted that he had met the young Jimmy Hendrix back in 1956, when he was aged just 13, in Macon, Georgia. There, it's suggested, the young Hendrix's fascination with the blues

prompted him to undergo some sort of initiation ceremony. With his parents frequently estranged, Hendrix did lead a nomadic lifestyle as a child, which led him to the Deep South. There, another Macon musician recalls him as a struggling, unexceptional musician who was transformed by this mysterious ceremony into a bluesman of shamanic powers, an event that would provide the impetus for "Voodoo Chile". His father always derided the story as nonsense but then, Hendrix as a child would have been too afraid as a child to disclose to his father that he had made a trip South without his knowledge and permission and, even as an adult, certainly too afraid to admit to him he'd been through an initiation ceremony.

Jimi Hendrix himself claimed to have actually seen voodoo practised. The rituals and beliefs of voodoo were a hangover from West African culture that had persisted in African-American communities and were especially pervasive on the Deep South blues scene; "You think this sort of thing is rubbish until it happens to you, then it's scary. Things like witchcraft, which is a form of exploration and imagination, have been banned by the establishment and called evil. It's because people are frightened to find out the full power of the mind."

However, that statement, evidence of the credulity that was grist to Hendrix's creativity, is arguably on a par with belief in UFOs rather than evidence on any deep-seated commitment or pivotal experience. It might also be an attempt to confer on Hendrix the black mark of authenticity, claim him as squarely one of the tragic, born-under-a-bad-sign bluesmen, à la Robert and Tommy Johnson, both of whom supposedly made Faustian pacts with the devil at country crossroads, exchanging their souls for their talent.

Hendrix was certainly taken with the notion of himself as a Voodoo Chile and, though it's not the only persona he projects through his music, it's among the most dominant, perhaps on the sheer strength of this, and "Voodoo Child (Slight Return)" alone. And "Voodoo Chile", in the lengthy, excursive form it takes on *Electric Ladyland*, is certainly a dazzling revisiting of the blues, harking back, as Charles Shaar Murray has put it, to the "spooky tranced-out delta moans of the 1920s": "Well the night I was born/I swear the moon turned a fire red." As the lyric develops, however, it conforms more to the sci-fi inspired psychedelic fancy of his own time and music, a science fiction topography of liquid gardens and red sands. Hendrix traverses decades of blues in minutes.

The supernaturalism of "Voodoo Chile" is at odds with the more feminised variety he'd pursued on "Have You Ever Been (To Electric Ladyland)" and, later on *First Rays Of The New Rising Sun*. Here, it's more masculine, assertive and boastful, a celebration of his own superpowers faintly akin to Muhammad Ali's boasts that he "done murdered a rock" and is so bad he "makes medicine sick". It's the darker side of infinite capability.

And yet, the jam session, as captured here, typifies the spirit of fun and joy in which much of *Electric Ladyland* was recorded – although on this occasion that spirit was marred by Noel Redding arriving at the studio and, finding the place full of hangers-on, bawling out Hendrix before storming out.

It was about seven in the morning by the time Hendrix, Mitch Mitchell and co began to kick into the groove on the third take of the track. Also present was Jack Cassady on bass and Traffic's Steve Winwood on organ, as well as a whole host of other musicians waiting out in the corridor, hoping to be able to sit in. Hendrix thrived on playing off organists – like Larry Young on "Nine To The Universe" or Mike Finnigan on "Still Raining, Still Dreaming". There's a particular rapport, however, with Winwood, whom Hendrix had several times tried and failed to work up the courage to ask if he'd care to join the Experience permanently.

Left to right: Carl Wayne, Stevie Winwood, Jimi Hendrix, John Mayall and Eric Burdon.

As Hendrix switches the ignition and the track rumbles into action, Steve Winwood matches his belligerent blues phraseology with a steady chatter of keyboard egged on by Mitchell's copious drumming and the argument is lively and sustained throughout, reaching a pitch of eloquence eight minutes in before a wonderful hiatus as Hendrix's guitar succumbs to an ear-splitting bout of feedback. The sounds of whoops and applause from the party people in the background were actually laid down separately a few days later.

LITTLE MISS STRANGE

Noel Redding's increasing sense of disenchantment with the Experience wasn't assuaged when he would arrive at the studio for sessions only to find that Hendrix hadn't bothered to turn up. It was on one such occasion that he decided to record "Little Miss Strange", a racy, acoustic-driven homage to an imaginary vampish seductress. Hendrix enjoyed the song, adding his own guitar overdub. Although the track pales and shrinks in the monumental company of *Electric Ladyland*, Hendrix insisted it was included on the album. He appreciated its quirkiness – and was maybe offering Redding a gesture of apology for messing him around.

LONG HOT SUMMER NIGHT

One of the earlier tracks to be sketched out and among the first to recorded at the Record Plant, "Long Hot Summer Night" isn't the most complex of lyrical conceits – Jimi's heart is "way down in a cold cold winter storm", estranged as he is from his woman. When she calls to tell him she's returning, however, his shack of misery is transformed and the thought of her return sends him into raptures, matched by a shimmering, ecstatic fretboard fadeout.

While Hendrix's guitar work is as effortlessly superlative as ever, it's his own harmonies, a sustained, heavenly host of falsetto, which really carry the track, a further sign of the confidence he was developing in his own vocal capabilities. Al Kooper, keyboardist with Bob Dylan, plays piano on the track. They went way back together to Hendrix's early days as Jimmy James in Greenwich Village. However, you have to strain to make out Kooper's contribution, which Hendrix, not the most inclusive or generous of producers, rather buries in the final mix.

COME ON (LET THE GOOD TIMES ROLL)

This cover of Earl King's rock'n'roll composition is a moment of relative respite before the next giant musical leap forward. It showcases Hendrix as audiences were accustomed to hearing him live, taking a familiar, cherished rock classic, toying affectionately with it, then unleashing a guitar solo that drags it screaming into the psychedelic era at warp speed.

GYPSY EYES

The extent to which the Cherokee side of Jimi Hendrix's family and upbringing determined his make-up is often underestimated. It's reflected in the spiritual rhythms of songs like "Little Wing" or the instrumental "Pali Gap". During his unsettled childhood, he'd spent time living with his half Cherokee grandmother on a reservation, and was once thrown out of church for wearing the flamboyant, Native American clothes she made for him. She instilled in him a pride in, and a strong awareness of, his Cherokee background.

Hendrix's mother, Lucille, was from the Native American side of the family. Never especially healthy following a bout of pneumonia early in life, she was unable to look after little Jimmy properly as a child. Her marriage to Al, meanwhile, was a stormy one. He was patriarchal and authoritarian, she, despite her frail constitution and vulnerability to bouts of depression, a loud, party-loving soul. They had met and married following America's entry into the war. Jimmy was born in 1942 then Al and Lucille separated after the father returned from the war in 1945, reuniting briefly later in the decade to produce another son, Leon, in 1948. However, they were clearly incompatible and, by 1950 had separated for good. Al would take responsibility for his two boys, though for a while they would have to live with his sister Patricia, as he tried to find work. Lucille died in 1958; Al refused to allow Jimmy and Leon to attend the funeral.

"Gypsy Eyes" has the musical and lyrical feel of a horny paean to a hot-blooded babe who will answer all Hendrix's sexual needs. In actual fact, however, it's addressed to Lucille, and expresses a poignant and forlorn desire to reestablish contact with her free spirit, which he imagines to be roaming the highways.

As with John Lennon, Hendrix's fleeting contact with his mother only intensified his feelings for her, though in Hendrix's case she represented more of a romantic ideal than a strong memory, a figure who visited him in his dreams, like the one Hendrix spoke of having as a child. "My mother was being carried away on this camel. And there was a big caravan; she's saying 'Well, I'm not gonna see ya now' . . . two years after that she died . . . some dreams you don't forget."

In the song, which seems to be a musical recollection of that dream, Hendrix envisages his mother catching his eye and telling him she could love him, but "first I must make my getaway." Unlike Lennon, whose song "Mother" is still full of uncomprehending grief that his mater had abandoned him, Hendrix seems to understand why his own mother had to fly the nest, in order to be true to her nature. Finally, in the imaginary context of the song at least, Lucille makes good on her promise to Hendrix to come back for him and, in the soaring fade-out, an elated Jimi hollers a simple phrase conspicuously absent elsewhere in his songwriting; "I love you . . ."

Owing to the personal nature of this song, feeling he owed something to the memory of his late mother, Hendrix was determined to get it absolutely right. He went through hundreds of takes, remixes and overdubs, to the terminal exasperation of Chas Chandler, who felt that Hendrix had gilded the lily once too often, and eventually took it as his cue to walk out on the star. However, while the song does feel heavily "processed", that only adds to its feeling of internal torment, twisting and writhing along life's freeway.

BURNING OF THE MIDNIGHT LAMP

The earliest track on Electric Ladyland to be recorded, "Burning Of The Midnight Lamp" was released in 1967, coupled with "The Stars That Play With Laughing Sam's Dice". Curiously, Hendrix later described this as "The best track we ever produced" and while it's hardly that, it certainly marks an excellent bridging point between the Axis and Ladyland eras.

The song showcases Hendrix's first use of wah-wah, a pedal device previously used by Frank Zappa and also by Eric Clapton on Cream's *Disraeli Gears*, but for which Hendrix would go on to create an entire dictionary of expression. Here, its blubbering cascades denote a "loneliness" that is "such a drag". It also features the strains of the harpsichord, whose use had been popularised on the Beatles' "Lucy In The Sky With Diamonds". He'd never played the instrument before, yet manages to pull off a suitably gothic, if rather stiff, performance to match the mood of the song, which reminds you of Miss Havisham in Dickens' *Great Expectations* alone in her mansion, cobwebs hanging from the candelabras.

Although the song seems, on the face of it, to be a lament for a lost love whose image stares at Hendrix from his "frowning wall", the track was actually written during a temporary bout of despair on his part, while travelling on a plane between L.A. and New York. He felt that the fortunes of the Experience were fading. Chafing against the limited expectations of the band, he felt himself condemned to go through the same, diminishing motions to a diminishing audience.

The song is despondent, almost hinting at suicide as Hendrix threatens to "blow my mind", but fortunately the way he would blow his mind and escape the rut he felt the Experience was in was through the groundbreaking and bond-breaking sonic experimentation of *Electric Ladyland*. The gospel harmonies here were provided by the Sweet Inspirations, Aretha Franklin's backing singers, led by Cissy Houston, mother of Whitney. They played their part gamely, but regarded the flamboyant, be-hatted Hendrix with Christian bewilderment.

RAINY DAY, DREAM AWAY

Due to play at a pop festival in Miami in May 1968, the Experience turned up only to find themselves in the middle of a downpour that saw the last day cancelled. Hendrix seems to have taken the news philosophically – he could probably have done with the break. He also took the opportunity to kick back and immortalise this non-event in song.

The easy-going mood of "Rainy Day, Dream Away" is emphasised by the way it stutters informally into action, with Hendrix coughing into the mic, before striking up a casual musical conversation with Freddie Smith on sax and Mike Finnigan on organ. Hendrix's phrasing is deceptively lackadaisical – the notes fall like droplets from his fingers but actually form intricate patterns. The song ambles amiably along in a reverie, before taking a left turn, then grinding dramatically to a halt as a thunderclap of feedback, dubbed in later, breaks overhead. Then, just as it's really about to get busy, it fades out to make way for . . .

1983 . . . (A MERMAN I SHOULD TURN TO BE) / MOON TURN THE TIDES . . . GENTLY, GENTLY AWAY

With this extraordinary, extended song suite conceived with Eddie Kramer, Hendrix truly established himself in the great tradition of "Afro futurists". These included Sun Ra, the jazz bandleader who declared that he had been born on Saturn, and who on pieces like "I'll Wait For You" and "Cosmic Explorer" simulated inter-galactic travel with his dazzling bursts of abstract synthesizer. They included also Miles Davis, who popularised the use of electronic instruments in jazz. Then there was George Clinton, who "arrived" onstage in a huge mothership. ("Who'd ever conceive of a nigger in a spaceship?" he used to laugh in interviews). Later would come Afrika Bambaata, Derrick May and A Guy Called Gerald, all pioneers in electro-funk and techno.

Hendrix himself was an avid devourer of science fiction paperbacks, which he often borrowed from Chas Chandler. And in matters of the paranormal, Jimi counted himself among the ranks of the non-sceptical.

There is a reason why so many black musicians seem to embrace futurism in music. It holds the promise of better places, of better things. Nostalgia-driven retroism often plays less well among black audiences as there's generally precious little in their collective past to evoke such warm feelings; it's the past of the civil rights movement, of inequality of opportunity, lack of recognition, social pariah status . . . and the present isn't so hot either. Conversely, occasional movements like Britpop smack suspiciously of a collective desire for a white-dominated pop past, with its airily innocent connotations of a time when life was less "complex" and black people were invisible.

Hendrix's music certainly reached out way beyond its era, in the distant hope that as-yet unoccupied decades like the 1980s and 1990s held better prospects. Here, he envisages himself and his lover making their escape from a perpetually war-torn and ecologically ruined world, taking to the sea in a machine of their own devising, in search of the lost utopia of Atlantis. Hendrix recalls the derision of his friends, literally echoing, in a scoffing slo-mo effect in his ears, who assure him it's impossible for a man to live and breathe under water, with Mitch Mitchell's stiff, militaristic backbeat providing a satirical accompaniment to their earthbound uptightness. They approach the shore, make love one last time, then take to the sea, accompanied by the recurring sound of buoy gong-bells and pealing seagulls (feedback effects achieved by Hendrix's earphones feeding back into the mic), and a riff that's reminiscent of the Animals' "House Of The Rising Sun". This is ironic, given that that track had been recorded in a single take, while ex-Animal Chas Chandler despaired at what he saw as the excessive studio dawdling involved in tracks like "1983".

As the suite bleeds into "Moon, Turn The Tides… Gently, Gently Away", Kramer and Hendrix brilliantly evoke, by means of phasing, backward taping and varispeed, a sense of amphibious descent, a darkening shade of submarine turquoise, of new forms of marine life zigzagging in shoals, peeking curiously into the cabin windows, of purple starfish darting in and out of the coral, giant sea-horses and electric eels torpedoing through the depths. Hendrix's Hawaiian-tinged guitar pickings suggest an idyll, but there's a worrying moment, sketched by Chris Woods' nervy flurries of flute and Mitch Mitchell's frantic percussion, as stress and turbulence seem to be taking their toll, with the deep sea divers in danger of succumbing to the bends. Then, a deeper calm as the danger passes and, in the new spirit of playful oceanic bliss, Hendrix picks up a bass guitar and plays a bubbling, intricate solo.

Finally, the mythical city of "Atlantis, full of cheer" becomes visible in the distance, and Hendrix and his lover make their concluding descent into the oceanic unknown.

The reverberations and implications of "1983…" have spread far and wide, from *Bitches Brew* to amorphous, modern musical forms like dub and ambient, affecting the music of Talk Talk, Robert Wyatt and many others. Its dream of a return to the womb-like succour of the ocean had a personal appeal for Hendrix. It's the ultimate drop-out, a fantasy act of disengagement for a man who, his rebellious nature subdued by a disciplinary upbringing, wasn't inclined to stay on land and fight. But this sublimely escapist trip has a universal pull as strong as the tide. Considering that Hendrix is regarded by some as the ultimate "cock rocker", it's one of the most "feminised" pieces of rock music ever created, with Hendrix, as the writer Simon Reynolds put it, "exploring the anima kingdom within his own soul", in defiance of the patriarchal "will of God and the grace of the King". At the time, it was to tracks like this that critics pointed when accusing Hendrix of contrivance and self-indulgence. True, it was fourteen hours in the making. Yet, by comparison with the computer processing techniques by which even the most traditional-sounding rock records are made in the twenty-first century, it ranks as a virtuoso feat of mixing board improvisation, in which sleight of hand was vital. "It was all done in one go," recalled Eddie Kramer. "We'd be flying around the board like lost flies." The result is a piece as impossible to simulate in real live conditions as was the undersea voyage it describes, a miraculous, one-off sound painting of Hendrix's imagination.

STILL RAINING, STILL DREAMING

On which Hendrix takes up from where he left off in the fade-out. The hoary old cliché that Hendrix "could make his guitar talk" probably finds its origins in "Still Raining, Still Dreaming", whose opening phrase sounds almost verbal, complete with exclamation and question marks. Hendrix described the sort of jamming he engages in here with organist Mike Finnigan and percussionist Larry Faucett as "like making love to another musically". But there's no doubt about who's on top here. Hendrix's garrulous, increasingly frenzied wah-wah absolutely dominates the track, with Mike Finnigan barely able to make an impression in the midst of this spermatozoid guitar maelstrom. Guest drummer Buddy Miles, meanwhile, contents himself with pounding out a jaunty, singsong backbeat.

"Still Raining, Still Dreaming" is also significant in that it's the first track recorded under the "Experience" banner to feature neither Mitch Mitchell nor Noel Redding. Mitchell was cool with this, Redding less so. As if oblivious to the discord, however, this is the most joyful piece on the album, Hendrix's face clearly split with an ear-to-ear grin throughout.

HOUSE BURNING DOWN

1968 was the year the world caught fire. Student demonstrations in Paris in the May were matched by scenes of protest and discord at the US Democratic Party convention. In April, Martin Luther King was assassinated on the balcony of a motel in Memphis, sparking off riots in 60 American cities. In June, Robert Kennedy, who some regarded as the youthful conscience of the Democratic Party, was gunned down at close range, his murder attributed to Palestinian-born Sirhan Sirhan. The war in Vietnam, which had already seen Buddhist monks make human torches of themselves by way of protest, intensified with the Tet Offensive, while unknown to the American public, members of Charlie Company, 11th Brigade went on a killing spree in the village of Mai Lai. Soviet tanks rolled into Prague to put down the tentative reforms of the Dubcek regime. Everywhere you looked, the flowers of 1967 were being trampled underfoot or blowtorched.

It was in the fiery light of such global affairs that "House Burning

As the war in Vietnam intensified, so did the anti-war movement back home. Yet not until 1968 did Hendrix shift from his originally pro-war stance.

Down" was written. Hendrix was especially upset at the rioting among African-American communities, which seemed especially self-defeating and ironic, given Martin Luther King's avowed pacifism.

The sentiments to "House Burning Down" are pacific, though Hendrix himself was not exactly a pacifist. As an ex-paratrooper, he was a supporter of the Vietnam War right up until 1968. And, like John Lennon, that other great peacenik in rock, Hendrix had violence in him. A man who tended to bottle tensions and frustrations up, he would occasionally erupt. In January 1968, for instance, in the middle of a typically gruelling and crammed European tour, he drank himself senseless and smashed a hotel room in Gothenburg to pieces. Women, too, could be the victims of his suppressed wrath. Once, engaged in a three-in-a-bed romp, he famously freaked out and started banging the heads of his female companions together.

"House Burning Down" is, then, paradoxical. On the one hand, its message is a very simple one, delivered over a tango-like rhythm – just cool it, people. With the other, huge and dexterous left hand, however, he unleashes one of the most incendiary guitar performances of his life, a conflagration of treble panning back and forth across the speakers like a firestorm, as the sky turns a "hell-fire red". Then, with the song done, there's another Eddie Kramer-assisted volley of electricity – Hendrix sustains a fireball-like riff which seems to subside, then, as if deciding there's business unfinished, rears up again and delivers one last awesome, eviscerating gash.

Some people have suggested that this coda was intended to signify the feline rage of the Black Panthers, who at this point were beginning to take an interest in Hendrix. He acknowledged them. "They come to the concerts and I sort of feel them there – it's not a physical thing, but a mental ray. It's a spiritual thing." However, he fell well short of endorsing them, even comparing them to "sheep" in one interview. Yet there's a baring of the teeth, a hint in "House Burning Down" that Hendrix, though never overtly political, was becoming conscious, albeit at a subliminal level. His patience, like that of the disaffected all over the world, the refuseniks and peaceniks, as well as his fellow African-Americans, was wearing thin.

A Buddhist monk sets fire to himself in protest at the Vietnam war.

ALL ALONG
THE WATCHTOWER

Bob Dylan's 1967 album *John Wesley Harding*, the first album following his period of reclusiveness and recuperation from a motorbike accident the previous year, stood in deliberately stark contrast to its musical times. If *Electric Ladyland* was, according to its critics, the most over-wrought album of the late 1960s, then *John Wesley Harding* was the most under-wrought. Recorded in just six hours, and consisting principally of acoustic instruments, it felt like an ascetic response to the baroque, flamboyant music scene that Dylan had helped create and now, it seemed, disowned.

One of the album's key tracks was "All Along The Watchtower". It obliquely alludes to Bob Dylan's frustrations with his management and with CBS, whom he felt were offering him a royalty rate that was far from commensurate with his status. It features a stand-off between the "joker" and the "thief", with the joker complaining of businessmen who drink his wine, feeding off him but refusing to give him his due. The thief cautions him not to concern himself with these material matters, that they are above that sort of thing, and that, with the "hour getting late" there are higher, and more urgent matters to contend with. This is signalled by the ominous approach, visible from the watchtower, of two riders and a gale that's beginning to pick up. Dylan delivers the song in the same cryptic and unprepossessing manner as the rest of the album, like a stranger shambling out of the backwoods and handing you a single tarot card to contemplate before shambling off again.

Jimi Hendrix was a freak for Bob Dylan, especially his later work, with the sheer colour and variation of its biblical/surrealist/psychedelic/symbolist lyrical overtones. Dylan was, after all, prior even to the Beatles, the author of "attitude" in rock music. Hendrix carried a Dylan songbook about his person at all times and frequently dipped into it for lyrical inspiration. Early in his career, he had covered "Like A Rolling Stone", delivering the song with concussive impact at Monterey. Somewhat backhandedly, Hendrix would also claim Dylan as the man who gave him the confidence to take up singing. "I thought, you must admire that guy for having that much nerve to sing so out of key." If Dylan could do it, then why not Jimi?

Hendrix would certainly have identified with Dylan's grievances with the music business, as his dealings with Ed Chalpin, who held him to a contract he's signed in 1965 for an advance of one dollar, and his current manager, the slippery Mike Jeffery, would attest. However, in the end, he seems to have heeded the advice of the thief, waiving confrontation and settling instead for cultivating his muse.

Other groups, notably the Byrds, had covered Dylan's songs, successfully fleshing them out and adding their own colour and tone. The transformation wrought by Hendrix on the original is something else again. He takes the charcoal miniature of the original and makes of it a full-blown, wide-screen, Technicolor, Sergio Leone-type epic, bringing out all its inherent drama in an intricately detailed masterpiece. The opening, with its acoustic fanfare and sonic equivalent of a zoom lens close-up of a rattlesnake in the Mojave Desert, establishes the parched landscape on which the song's action takes place, before Hendrix thunders in like a one-man posse. His delivery of the opening line, "There must be some kind of way out of here" is as deeply felt as any in his repertoire. His voice almost cracks, as if he is momentarily distracted by just how much the sentiment speaks to his own depths of feeling.

Bob Dylan, whom Hendrix idolised for his attitude, his lyrics – and his off-key singing.

The centrepiece of "Watchtower" is in its series of solos, devastating and distinct like four horsemen of some guitar apocalypse. The first is "straight", the second a looping slide, its bottleneck effects achieved with the aid of a cigarette lighter, the third a *danse macabre* of wah-wah, the fourth a thrilling gallop. Then, as the "wind began to howl" so does Hendrix's electric lady, a sky-bound, elongated shriek as the song fades to black.

Dylan himself would later acknowledge the power of Hendrix's version and, in performing a more heavy-duty arrangement of it on his 1974 album *Before The Flood*, practically conceded that Hendrix had made the song his own. "Strange how when I sing it I always feel it's a tribute to him in some kind of way," he said.

"All Along The Watchtower" was one of the songs that made Hendrix a favourite among troops in Vietnam. Broadcast over pirate radio systems set up by G.I.s fed up with Armed Forces Radio, its firepower all too vividly matched the reality of their own heated circumstances. Described by critic Tony Palmer as "an assault which must be like the roaring one hears before being disintegrated by an exploding hydrogen bomb", it is among the most thrilling few minutes in rock music's entire canon. Yet on this album there was still better to come.

VOODOO CHILD (SLIGHT RETURN)

A film crew from ABC filmed the Experience running through the fourteen or so takes of this song, during which it took on its final shape, shading and mass as Hendrix added new elements into the mix. Unfortunately, the footage was later stolen from ABC's archives.

This reprise is a different evolution altogether from the earthy, relatively organic blues jam of "Voodoo Chile". "Slight" is hardly the word. It's as if the braggadocio blues man of the first take has slunk away to brood, then returned, more fearsome than before, powers multiplied and having taken on a newer, supernatural form. The intro hoves in with a burgeoning, karate-funk riff, like some extra-terrestrial threshing machine, emitting a wah-wah warning signal, before exploding into being, a being of the heaviest, purest, most uncut metal.

"Well I stand up next to a mountain/And I chop it down with the edge of my hand", brags Hendrix, the rock god in full effect, hurling down verbal and musical thunderbolts. The sheer density assails you, rises to boiling point, until midway through the song seems to burst into flames, a volcanic eruption precipitating a stream of lava. Noel Redding seems to be crushed like a fleeing Pompeian, his bass, perhaps unfairly, barely registering in the Hendrix production, while even Mitch Mitchell, flailing at full strength, makes a negligible impact, the mere sound of leaves brushing against a window pane in the middle of a tornado. Hendrix's guitar howls in an almost malevolent, lupine ecstasy, pouring it on with a red-hot relish, until the devastation is complete.

"Voodoo Child" raised the volume and temperature of rock music forever. Much as world events had rendered obsolete the tentative optimism of 1967, so "Voodoo Child" reduced to black cinders the mellow yellow vibe of poppy psychedelia in 1968. Even the Beatles, studio innovators as they were, would no longer be able to compete in this new era of super-heavyweight pyromania. George Harrison's gently weeping guitar was no match for this.

Of course, it could be argued that this was a bad thing, that all that Hendrix had done here was, in effect, to give birth to one of his most unfortunate offshoots, heavy metal. Certainly, the megaton riffola here would "inspire" legions of tight-trousered, screeching would-be axe warriors in the 1970s and 1980s to inflict on us endless fiddly and over-amplified guitar solos. Thanks a lot, Jimi. However, while they might have matched Hendrix for volume, they would never match him for substance.

This was not merely music for spotty, longhaired adolescents to dream their self-aggrandizing dreams of spurious conquests to (although, doubtless, many spotty adolescents *did* use Hendrix that way). There was a context to Voodoo Child – 1968 was the year of Black Power.

At the Mexico Olympics of that year, African-American athletes, assisted by the high altitude conditions, were setting astonishing new records. Bob Beamon leapt 8.90m in the long jump, hurtling so far that someone had to fetch a tape to measure the distance by hand, the electronic device having proven inadequate. And Tommie Smith, the 200m sprinter, won his final in a belief-beggaring world's best time of 19.83 seconds. He and John Carlos (who came third) entered the stadium shoeless and, as they stood on the podium during the national anthem, raised leather glove fists aloft in a memorable and courageous act of defiance that would cost both men their sporting careers. "Voodoo Child" is the soundtrack to this defiance, not so much a declaration but a terrifying representation of Black Power. Hendrix would later announce the song as "Harlem's national anthem" and

"America's national anthem" and dedicate it to "our friends in West Africa". It represents the growing anger and assertiveness of African-Americans, a people on the point of coming into their own. Hendrix had once been feared and leered at as a symbol of black sexual potency. This, however, was potency of a larger and different order. It is, perhaps, the most potent rock record ever made.

"Voodoo Child" was released as a single following Hendrix's death in 1970. Many people, therefore, might have come to the understandable, though chronologically incorrect, conclusion that this was Hendrix's valedictory gesture; "I'll see you in the next world, don't be late", the final, glorious combustion of a genius who had grown too large for this world and was moving on. In this context, the way the song stutters unexpectedly to a halt, when it feels like it could have raged on a good deal longer, is truly poignant.

BAND OF GYPSYS

Recorded	October 1966 – April 1967 at De Lane Lea, CBS & Olympic Studios.
Produced by	Chas Chandler.
Engineered by	Dave Siddle, Eddie Kramer and Mike Ross.
Musicians:	Jimi Hendrix (lead vocals, backing vocals, guitar, handclaps, piano), Noel Redding (bass, backing vocals), Mitch Mitchell (drums, tambourine, backing vocals, cowbell).

WHO KNOWS
MACHINE GUN
CHANGES
POWER TO LOVE
MESSAGE TO LOVE
WE GOTTA LIVE TOGETHER

BURNING DESIRE
HEAR MY TRAIN A COMIN'
(LAST TWO TRACKS FROM
 LIVE AT THE FILLMORE EAST)

The story behind the *Band Of Gypsys* album begins in 1965, before The Jimi Hendrix Experience were dreamt of, back in a simpler, innocent era when earsplitting feedback was considered an aberration, when musicians stored their guitars carefully away after concerts, and used their teeth to smile genially to the camera rather than to play their instruments, and were routinely ripped off by kindly, paternal managers who bound them to contracts that would appall a galley slave.

In fairness, Hendrix himself does not come out of the story shrouded with any credit for either his probity or business acumen. In 1965, while playing with Curtis Knight & the Squires, Hendrix and his band leader were introduced to producer Ed Chalpin, head of PPX Enterprises, who signed them up to exclusive recording contracts. Hendrix, anxious for the chance to get into a studio, signed up at once for the sum of one dollar by way of an advance and a one per cent royalty rate. In his eagerness, he omitted to point out to Chalpin that he had already signed a similar deal with another producer, Juggy Murray, to record for R&B stable Sue Records.

Hendrix (far right) in the mid-Sixties, with Curtis Knight and the Squires.

Hendrix did record with Knight and the Squires under the auspices of Chalpin, but their singles bombed and Hendrix would soon tire of knocking out cover versions every night. He upped and made off for New York to form Jimmy James & The Blue Flames, settling in Greenwich Village before being duly taken on by Chas Chandler, who bought out the Sue Records contract and whisked him off to England. Hendrix, however, never bothered to tell him about his deal with Chalpin.

Chalpin, however, did not forget about Hendrix and, in 1967, when he read of the success of his former charge, with whom he had lost contact in late 1965, he launched legal proceedings in the hope of making good, and then some, on his one dollar investment. With Curtis Knight volunteering as a witness to the signing of the contract, Chalpin also released a couple of albums as spoilers to *Axis: Bold as Love* – *Get That Feeling* and *Flashing*, cobbled together from session tapes made during Hendrix's days as a Squire. Capitol Records, who now put their weight behind Chalpin's case, issued these. Perhaps as part of a misguided effort to sort the matter out personally, Hendrix actually approached both Chalpin and Curtis Knight during 1967, and even laid down guitar and bass parts for them in a studio session.

Eventually, in July 1968, an agreement was reached that, in addition to Chalpin receiving a percentage of royalty payments on the Experience's first three albums, Hendrix would deliver his follow-up to *Electric Ladyland* to Capitol, as compensation.

This would turn out to be the *Band Of Gypsys* LP. Hendrix's life was in turmoil during this period, caught as he was between the twin commitments of building a new studio and trying to rediscover/reinvent himself in the rural retreat of upstate New York, where he assembled a large group of musicians and spoke vaguely of inaugurating something he called "Electric Church Music". Caught between manager Mike Jeffery's anxiety to reform the Experience and the siren lure of his African-American roots, Hendrix began to feel that he owed it to himself to distance himself from the rock circus. He had disbanded the Experience, although he would retain the services of Mitch Mitchell. He muttered that he "didn't want to be a clown any more".

In the event, the *Band Of Gypsys* project and live album turned out to be a pretty reasonable deal for all concerned. It meant that Hendrix didn't have to give over the eventual recordings from his cherished *First Rays* sessions. It would enable him to give vent to the musical direction he had contemplated over the summer of 1969. Moreover, it would be over and done with in one night of work, featuring as it did material culled from two concerts played back-to-back at the Fillmore East on New Year's Eve, 1969, the second one finishing at 8 a.m. on New Year's Day. Ed Chalpin and Capitol would get their album while Mike Jeffery, having disposed of this contractual obligation, could concentrate on getting Hendrix back on the rock track.

Yet Hendrix was not happy in himself about the situation. He resented having to give Chalpin any more than the single dollar he had received from him. He was unhappy also that he would have no artistic control over either the production or packaging of the *Band Of Gypsys* album. He held back certain new songs that he did not choose to showcase, such as "Ezy Ryder", and insisted that two Buddy Miles songs be among the six featured on the original album – "Changes" and "We Gotta Live Together".

Buddy Miles was the drummer with the Band Of Gypsys and Billy Cox, Hendrix's dependable old army pal, was on bass. Miles had already enjoyed success in his own right, and would have regarded himself as on equal musical terms with Jimi. He enjoyed the acclaim of musicians such as Mike Bloomfield, who had dubbed him "superspade." To the dismay of some who have heard the *Band Of Gypsys* album, Miles did not shrink from adding generous vocal contributions of his own – indeed, if you didn't know better, you might almost mistake Miles for the band leader, and Hendrix for a shy but brilliant up-and-coming prospect within his line-up. Miles exuded a robust self-confidence that was foreign to Hendrix's nature. Along with Cox, he laid down a more soulful rhythm for Hendrix to work off; laid-back, grooved and lacking the maniacal tendencies of Mitch Mitchell.

Billy Cox, Hendrix's old army pal who eventually joined him on bass.

Mike Jeffery hated Miles. He asked awkward questions about where the money due the Gypsys was going, even though Miles himself was on a salary. Jeffery was also concerned at the alarming number of black people with whom Hendrix was now surrounding himself musically. In America, in particular, some white kids would be loath to go to see Hendrix if it meant being surrounded by a majority black audience. There were whispers in Jimi's ear. As guitarist Johnny Winter said, "The white guys and managers would say, 'Don't play with these niggers, man… get the cute English guys back'."

Yet the daft thing was, by nature, Hendrix had always been genuinely colour-blind. In his own, sci-fi terms, he considered himself to be an earthling. He had always been used to the company of white folks, both growing up, in the army and during his working life. He hadn't appeared to mind too much all that "wild man of rock" stuff. He'd initially spurned the advances of the Black Panthers, even bracketing them with the Ku Klux Klan. He'd displayed an indifference to cultivating a traditional soul/R&B audience – indeed, that was what he was trying to get away from – and revelled in the company of the likes of Eric Clapton, who would later speak as fondly of Enoch Powell as he had of Hendrix. Hendrix was the sort of black man a 1960s white man could almost feel comfortable with.

However, correcting voices began to whisper in his ear. Among the first was that of Ram John Holder, a West Indian whom he first met in New York and later in London. He harangued Hendrix for putting up so passively with the "wild man of Borneo" bullshit that the tabloid press had hurled at him, the sort of epithets in which his own management had colluded. And, in accordance with his passive nature, Hendrix swallowed the diatribe, head bowed, a little shamefaced.

Then, after the death of Martin Luther King Jnr and the political firestorms of 1968, Hendrix couldn't help but be touched by the heat. His interests in jazz and soul music also represented an alternative to the rock spectacle he increasingly tired of, a new place to go musically. Figures like Buddy Miles, angry and bigging up the power of soul, would have his ear more and more.

In September 1969, Hendrix gigged up in Harlem in an effort to bring his music "back home". Whitey, meanwhile, in the form of Mike Jeffery, was cutting a more conspicuously devilish figure. That same month, Hendrix had been abducted from his apartment by four heavies, bundled into the back of a car, blindfolded and driven off to a remote, bare-floored building. There, he'd been threatened with violence. However, following a commotion and an altercation he could only hear, his blindfold was removed and he was staring up a concerned-looking Mike Jeffery and members of his staff, Jimi's apparent "rescuers". But how had they known he'd needed rescuing? He was convinced that Jeffery, posing as his protector, was putting the frighteners on him. If Hendrix wasn't 100% sure about the Band Of Gypsys, the fact that Jeffery voiced misgivings about the project only made him more determined to pursue it.

GRAHAM FELT THAT THE THEATRICS WERE IMPEDING HENDRIX'S PLAYING

For all of this, Hendrix was not finding it easy to achieve the sounds of blackness he envisaged. Early rehearsal sessions for the *Band Of Gypsys* album and concert were protracted, shapeless affairs, with Jimi and cohorts grinding out a rough but unready R&B sound that didn't cohere well. Although, as the album amply evinces, the band *did* hit a groove, in his heart of hearts, Hendrix must have realised that it wasn't just to fulfil a legal obligation that he was making this album. It was part of an effort to conscript him to the black cause and Hendrix, despite his military past, baulked at conscription of any kind. The Band Of Gypsys were cool – but they weren't the future.

Despite the fraternal air among the musicians and despite the call-and-response nature of the songs, on the night Hendrix appears primarily to have been concerned about his own playing. During the first set, he'd gone

out and given it the full theatrical works, which went down hugely well. However, the Fillmore's Bill Graham, mindful of the fact that this was a recording as well as a performance, poured lukewarm waters on Hendrix's efforts. Graham felt that the theatrics were impeding Hendrix's playing and told him so. Although crestfallen, Hendrix took the criticism to heart and played the following set practically as immobile as a statue. With the album in the can, he then unleashed an encore full of tongue, teeth, bump and grind. He'd said he "didn't want to be a clown", but when it came to this sort of showmanship, it seemed he just couldn't help himself.

The late Sixties saw a growth in Black Power militancy with which Hendrix increasingly sympathized.

Critical response to the album was mixed. *Melody Maker*'s critic sniffed that, to his mind, it was "rather old fashioned by today's freak standard." The album would go on to be Hendrix's second best seller to date. However, the Band Of Gypsys did not last very long. Against the wishes of Mike Jeffery, they had booked to play a massive concert for the Vietnam Moratorium Committee in Madison Square Garden. Prior to the gig, Hendrix was given some especially virulent LSD that had an immediate and deleterious effect on him. Quivering and nauseous, he only lasted two numbers. The next day, Jeffery used the debacle as an excuse to fire Buddy Miles. Miles, in turn, would later assert that it had been Jeffery who had nobbled Hendrix with the dodgy LSD. Hendrix, however, did not make any effort to overturn his manager's decision.

Certainly, Jeffery was happy that the Band Of Gypsys were no more, and to announce the reformation of the Jimi Hendrix Experience. However, while happy to play with Mitch Mitchell, Hendrix refused to play alongside the hapless Noel Redding. Once again, it fell to others than Hendrix to break the bad news to Noel. Billy Cox retained his berth on bass, and this Gypsys/Experience hybrid would constitute the trio within which Hendrix would make the bulk of his final studio recordings.

(The following tracks appeared on *Band Of Gypsys*, the original album released in 1969, and/or *Live At The Fillmore East*, the 2-CD album that featured other songs taken from the same New Years Eve concerts).

WHO KNOWS

This track, the opener, established the sort of rolling, laid-back, funkier groove that Billy Cox and Buddy Miles would provide for Jimi. It's an initially odd experience for those accustomed to Mitchell's all-guns-blazing drum assault and Redding's hammered-down bass, and the intro allows us time to acclimatize.

The lyric is a blues lamentation, with Buddy Miles, a little distractingly, acting as a human echo to Hendrix. Somewhat dazed and confused and uncertain of his bearings, Jimi finds himself back in town, unable to track down his "baby", whom, he is distressed to suspect, has been so bold as to take advantage of the 1960s sexual liberation – indeed, has "spread the magic" in Hendrix's own bed. Her devilish nature is confirmed in the lyrical outtro, as she "walks down the street singing" without a care for Hendrix, whom she still has in her vampish grip; "she got chains attached to my head".

What then follows, the hair in this particular voodoo soup, is perhaps the worst musical interlude on any Hendrix record. On the lyrical cue of "singin'", Buddy Miles takes it upon himself to embark on a scat odyssey. Although a decent crooner, superior to Hendrix in many ways, scat proves to be well beyond Miles' range. Imagine one of *Monty Python's* screeching hags attempting to imitate a thrush and you've some idea of the awfulness of his vocalising. One can only imagine that it was the deep fraternal bond forged between Hendrix and Miles that prevented Jimi from shuddering openly. Thankfully, the episode is soon over, and Hendrix embarks on a lengthy, growling solo that goes some way to expunging the trauma. The ovation the Band Of Gypsys receive suggests he succeeded.

MACHINE GUN

Hendrix performed two versions of this at the Fillmore East concerts – it's hard to decide which of them is the more towering. "Machine Gun" is the centrepiece of *Band Of Gypsys* and the reason why purchase of the album is mandatory.

Hendrix was all turned around on the Vietnam issue. In mid-1967, the US Army had actually invited the Jimi Hendrix Experience to take part in a promotional broadcast as part of a campaign to get young people to enlist and replenish the ranks of American troops fighting in the Far East. The band agreed and, following a broadcast of "Purple Haze" and a brief interview with Hendrix, DJ Harry Harrison weighed in with an incongruous pitch; "It's your future, it's your decision, choose army!"

By 1969, however, like many fellow Americans, Hendrix was profoundly disaffected with the Vietnam campaign. "Machine Gun" is among his most musically erudite gestures of dissent.

At Fillmore East, Hendrix announced the song thus; "This next song is dedicated to all the troops fighting in Harlem, Chicago and, oh yes, Vietnam.

A little thing called 'Machine Gun'." With drummer Miles simulating the rat-tat-tat of automatic rifle fire, Hendrix sets forth, gorge rising. He speaks for not one soldier but all the frontline warriors, on both sides of the conflict, continually torn apart by bullets, yet rising up only to be scythed down again; "Evil man make me kill you/Evil man make you kill me/ Even though we're families apart."

Hendrix, now an altogether different kind of spokesman for the army, predicts, accurately, to the "evil man" that his rain of violence will only blow back on him; "Same way you shoot me down, baby/ You'll be going just the same with three times the pain . . and yourself to blame."

What really makes "Machine Gun", however, is its solo, in which Hendrix deploys his entire arsenal of effects, including Fuzz Face, wah-wah, Univibe and Octavia to paint a picture that sonically matches Picasso's "Guernica" in scope, range and intensity. His electric vocabulary of growls, wails, sighs, bends and visceral passion is used here to express anger, lamentation and flesh-ripping anguish. Hendrix's playing tortuously yet beautifully evokes a chaotic welter of tribulations – hot metal tearing through bodies, the blood-drenched earth screaming, aircraft strafing the foliage with Agent Orange.

Hendrix would feature the song throughout 1970, often dedicating the track to the victims at Kent State University, where four students were shot dead by the National Guard at an antiwar protest.

Hendrix's impassioned and hi-tech guitar playing uniquely conveyed the horrors of modern warfare in Vietnam.

This is the sort of Hendrix track that his many imitators were never able to get a handle on. Indeed, among its nearest musical relations is 1979's "Careering" by Public Image Ltd, John Lydon's take on the Irish situation, complete with Hendrix-style machine-gun effects and a stark ambience of unrelenting violence.

CHANGES

At Hendrix's insistence, two Buddy Miles tracks were featured on the original *Band Of Gypsys* album. "Changes" is a simple lament for a guy whose baby left him, sending him into mental turmoil, and slows and transforms into a gospel-style audience participation number. Hendrix provides old-school, souped-up R&B rhythms, then pulls out a protracted wah-wah solo from the middle drawer before politely receding into the background like an agnostic at a church service as Miles leads the crowd in a chant of "Everything's gonna be all right."

111

POWER TO LOVE

See Chapter Six, *South Southern Delta*.

MESSAGE TO LOVE

See Chapter Six, *South Southern Delta*.

WE GOTTA LIVE TOGETHER

This second Miles-penned track is in a similar vein to "Changes", with Miles again on lead vocals and Jimi chiming in. Once again the audience are invited to sing along, yet while this fraternal arm-linking is all very laudable, what really makes the track is Hendrix's tremendous solo, a quite gratuitous burst of electro-static energy which he then abruptly abandons, as if he is suddenly remembering his manners.

BURNING DESIRE

A track Hendrix worked on throughout November 1969, "Burning Desire" seems to have been developed from a snipping of "Fire" and overlaps extensively with "Come Down Hard On Me", into which it briefly transforms during this performance. A number of changes in tempo and direction indicate that this song had still to go through its own developmental process before settling into a final form. Although "Burning Desire" is sensual, it's very much in the hue of later Hendrix. There was a seriousness now even to his amorousness.

HEAR MY TRAIN A COMIN'

Along with "Red House", this was Hendrix's greatest home-baked blues offering. Although he'd been playing around with the track as far back as 1967, it was only towards the end of his career that it became a regular live warhorse.

"Hear My Train A Comin'" is Hendrix's homage to his own sense of destiny. He once introduced the song onstage thus. "It's about a cat running around town and his old lady, she don't want him around and a whole lot of people from across the tracks are putting him down. And nobody don't want to face up to it but the cat has something, only everybody's against him 'cause the cat might be a bit different. So he goes on the road to be a voodoo child, come back to be a magic boy."

No prizes for guessing who the "cat" is, then. Up until the age of 24, Hendrix had indeed been just another soul session musician bumming around the circuit, making no headway with his music but leading a transient life, enduring jibes for his appearance, wrapped up in his own shyness, almost perversely absorbed by his instrument. Whether his sense of being persecuted was real or imagined, these were deeply frustrating times for one of rock's most flamboyant and distinctive individualists, forced to stay in the back line on the chitlin' circuit, wear a tux and run through the same silly dance steps as everybody else. Only after Chas Chandler invited him over to England was he able to come back to America a "magic boy".

While it was ironic that his "train" of destiny to freedom should have taken him all the way from his vast homeland, the land of opportunity, to

the pokey back alleyways of swinging London, it was doubly ironic that by 1969, Hendrix sought the next plane of his destiny back out west in the country that had originally been so indifferent towards him, looking to shed the pop trappings that had skyrocketed him to fame. Now, his song of freedom rang out in San Diego, Woodstock and L.A.

The Fillmore East version of "Hear My Train A Comin'" is not the definitive one to be found on the album *Blues*. Here, as there, Hendrix's delivery of the song simmers with a raging hope that good fortune was coming round the mountain, ready to sweep him off his itchy feet and onto the next station in his life. While Hendrix was often prey to an almost overwhelming sense of gloom and hopelessness in his final months, it's good to know that a part of him was still driven by a belief in his own continuing and unstoppable evolution.

FIRST RAYS OF THE NEW RISING SUN

Recorded	October 1966 – April 1967 at De Lane Lea, CBS & Olympic Studios.
Produced by	Chas Chandler.
Engineered by	Dave Siddle, Eddie Kramer and Mike Ross.
Musicians:	Jimi Hendrix (lead vocals, backing vocals, guitar, handclaps, piano), Noel Redding (bass, backing vocals), Mitch Mitchell (drums, tambourine, backing vocals, cowbell).

FREEDOM

IZABELLA

NIGHT BIRD FLYING

ANGEL

ROOM FULL OF MIRRORS

DOLLY DAGGER

EZY RYDER

DRIFTING

BEGINNINGS

STEPPING STONE

MY FRIEND

STRAIGHT AHEAD

HEY BABY (NEW RISING SUN)

EARTH BLUES

ASTRO MAN

IN FROM THE STORM

BELLY BUTTON WINDOW

The years from 1967 to 1970 packed in a higher concentration of rock history, both highs and lows, than entire subsequent musical decades – and so it was to prove with Hendrix. The final months of his life, in particular, constituted a period of immense stress, activity, upheaval and re-evaluation.

Mitch Mitchell was still in the picture, musically, unlike Noel Redding, whom Hendrix had insisted should make way for Hendrix's ex-army buddy Billy Cox. There would be a shift in tone – if the Experience's earliest recordings sometimes thrived on a frenetic tension, as if all three instrumentalists were in a race to reach the end of the song first, now the air was more laid-back and pacific, as Hendrix sought solace and scanned the skies awaiting the return of his muse.

It was small wonder that he yearned for respite. There were many competing banes to Hendrix's life prior to the commencement of recording work on First Rays... In addition to an unsettled line-up, a drugs bust in Toronto and the Ed Chalpin lawsuit, there were the frustrations of the new state-of-the-art studio, Electric Lady in Greenwich Village. Mike Jeffery had persuaded him to set this up to reduce the astronomical fees he was running up at the Record Plant, give him the freedom to record as and when he pleased, and afford him a fixed asset which he could rent out to other musicians.

Unfortunately, construction problems hampered the building of the studio. Extensive soundproofing was required to offset the noise from a nearby subway tunnel, and the entire place was flooded out when workers hit an underground stream. Furthermore, the Mafia, who had headquarters nearby, were not too pleased that their hitherto discreet location was about to suffer the heat of the F.B.I, buzzing around a known rock hangout in search of a drugs bust. They informed Hendrix that their displeasure had been incurred.

Hendrix, like many other artists, was also beginning to resent the way his financial affairs were being handled. He wondered about Mike Jeffery, the dubious Bahamas account into which his monies were squirreled and the unfairness of his royalty rate. However, he could never quite bring himself to confront Jeffery, a tenacious cookie who had few scruples when it came to keeping his talons in his cash cow, and could be a pretty scary guy when he wanted to be. For Jeffery's part, he was concerned at Hendrix's increasing association with the Black Power movement, as well as his gradual drift towards a jazzier direction, away from the pop and rock formula that Jeffery regarded as a winning one.

Jimi's appearances at various festivals in 1969 and 1970, and at Woodstock in particular, added grist to his legend, but they were fraught affairs, both of which saw him appear onstage well after even hippie bedtime. At the Isle Of Wight festival, he played a chaotic, distracted set in the chilly pre-dawn air which left many erstwhile British fans regarding this skeletal figure, lost in a jamming reverie, and wondering what had become of "their" Jimi, Mr Purple Haze. A festival at Puttgarden in Germany in September shortly afterwards, meanwhile, suffered shades of Altamont, broken up by bikers and anarchists, with bassist Billy Cox falling victim to the same fate as had Hendrix on the last Band Of Gypsys gig – his drink being spiked with LSD.

If Hendrix live had become a heavy and wearisome proposition for some, however, Hendrix in the studio was not so far removed from his 1967 self, circa *Axis: Bold As Love*. He had mooted *First Rays Of The New Rising Sun* as a double album back in January 1969. Its working title had been *People, Hell And Angels*. The idea would be to not so much to take up where *Electric Ladyland* had left off – there are no "1983"-style exercises in oceanic soundscaping – but to consolidate (conliquidate, even) and reflect on where he'd been and where he hoped to head to next, musically. Even the conservative Mike Jeffery could not have objected to the lilting likes of "Angel", while the bawdy "Dolly Dagger" was cast in a recognizable Hendrix mould.

Musically, *First Rays . . .* would be more mercurial and streamlined than previous Hendrix offerings, a lighter sound, lithe and soulful while still offering an entire index of possibilities which only Led Zeppelin would come close to emulating. The sanguine title is cruelly ironic, reflecting Hendrix's hopes for an ascent to a more tranquil plane, the heavy shit that came with rock superstardom a distant memory. The overwhelming theme on the album is of breakaway, be it via the "highway of desire" on "Ezy Ryder", or into the arms of his muse as on "Angel", soothing his fevered brow and fulfilling impossible longings.

Hendrix was working on material for the double album right up until August 24, 1970. Two nights later, four tracks were debuted at the official launch of Electric Lady studios. With its curvaceous decor, lush colour scheme and muted lights that Jimi could alter according to his mood, it provided the perfect ambience for his new incarnation. Like the interior of a flying saucer, it was a dream made real, the ideal pad for a new start. "It was the womb in which he was going to create," said Eddie Kramer.

Then, following the privations of the Isle Of Wight festival and the Billy Cox/LSD incident in Germany, Hendrix took refuge in London, moving about from apartment to hotel, still evading the subpoenas of Ed Chalpin and his lawyers, looking to tie up loose strands of business, look up old friends and perhaps make another attempt to rid himself from the management snares of Mike Jeffery. Among those who put up Jimi were Monika Danneman, a former ice skater with artistic ambitions who had become attached to him. She would later claim he had proposed marriage to her, though in those last days Hendrix made the same offer, on a whim, to a number of casual girlfriends.

The exact details of Hendrix's last days on earth, September 17 and 18, 1970, remain a little unclear, not least because of the late Monika Danneman's erratic and inconsistent testimony on the subject, which author Tony Brown took apart in his 1997 book *Hendrix: The Final Days*. Danneman always maintained that she and Jimi had spent an evening together at her apartment at the Samarkand hotel, where she cooked him a meal and they drank some wine. The next day, at about 11 a.m., she was unable to wake him and called for an ambulance, which arrived some 20 minutes later. She then discovered that a number of her Vesperax, a super-strength German

Monika Danneman, in whose apartment Hendrix choked to death. She committed suicide in 1996.

prescription sleeping tablet, were missing. According to Danneman, Hendrix was still alive at that point, but thanks to incompetent ambulance men placing him in the vehicle, together with the sluggishness of medical staff once he reached the hospital, he later died.

This version of events persisted for many years, with Jimi a victim of establishment indifference and Danneman casting herself as the distraught wife-to-be, fighting for her man's life to the end. She even blamed the Mafia for his demise. However, another picture has emerged from the altogether more consistent testimony of ambulance staff and police on the scene. When they found Hendrix, he was clearly dead and in an awful mess, with efforts to revive him only token. There is also uncertainty, arising from her own accounts, as to how soon Danneman actually did ring for an ambulance, having first been unable to rouse Hendrix.

There are further anomalies, including the mess of red wine in which the authorities found Hendrix to be immersed, and in which they assumed he had drowned as he choked on his own regurgitation. Yet his blood-alcohol level was relatively low. Brown's account begs numerous questions regarding Danneman, who just six days later agreed to a photo session in which she poses cheerfully among her paintings. However, in April 1996, a few months prior to the publication of Brown's book, Danneman committed suicide. Kathy Etchingham, who successfully brought a long-running libel lawsuit against Danneman, later gave her own, pithy summary of events: "[Hendrix] was in the wrong place, at the wrong time, with the wrong person. She was a nutter."

In the weeks prior to his death, Hendrix was in a poor way. Many who saw him in his last days commented on how ashen he looked. He seemed to have aged beyond his 27 years, his hair a scarecrow grey and his expression weathered. He was snorting (although not injecting) heroin, in a quandary with his management and musical direction, afraid that his talent was ebbing and given to morose predictions of his own, imminent demise. "I am not sure I will live to be 28 years old," he told a European reporter. To another journalist, Sharon Lawrence, he confided, just two days before he died: "I'm almost gone."

Yet, perilous as his state of mind and body was, Hendrix's death, though tragic, was not inevitable. The annals of VH-1's *Behind The Music* are crammed with rock stars who endured far darker chapters than Hendrix, and managed to come out the other side. Had he realised the strength of the tablets he took on the night of September 17, he might well have been with us today. His friend Eric Burdon was initially convinced Hendrix had committed suicide. He didn't: it was an accident. Which is why the death of, say, Billie Holiday or Jim Morrison was saddening, but the death of Hendrix is maddening.

And *First Rays...* was evidence of the life force that still shone in Hendrix. However, it was not issued in anything resembling the form its creator had intended until 1997. Prior to that time, for complicated contractual obligations, its various tracks were spread out across a series of posthumous releases, including *The Cry Of Love* and *Rainbow Bridge*. Many of the tracks remain unfinished, especially "Hey Baby (New Rising Sun)". Others had barely reached the drawing board stage, unborn embryos of songs with such tantalizing titles as "Heaven Has No Sorrow" and "Valley Of Neptune".

Jimi Hendrix's funeral, at Greenwood Cemetery in Renton, Washington on October 1, 1970.

But it has to be said that even had the album been completed, it's doubtful that it would have matched the Martian intensity of the masterpiece that was *Electric Ladyland*, or whether it would have been the first step on the part of a reborn alchemist to undreamt-of musical things. Nevertheless, it's an exquisite and at times deeply moving album, in that it amounts to the inadvertent last testament of a uniquely gifted man who still had so much more to say.

The activist Eldridge Cleaver of the Black Power movement, who courted Hendrix towards the end of his life.

FREEDOM

Featuring the sort of mercurial, funky guitar playing that was the hallmark of his final recordings, "Freedom" was road-tested on Hendrix's European and American tours of 1970. The wonderfully skewed opening gambit gives way to one of Hendrix's most rousing, anthemic numbers. The air-punching "freedom" chant comes courtesy of Hendrix's friends Arthur and Albert Allen, the Ghetto Fighters, and is emphatically underscored by thunderous piano courtesy of Hendrix himself. With its adrenalin-pumping energy, it's a song that could be put to any number of political ends, from the anti-Vietnam war protesters to the increasingly militant civil rights struggle.

The lyric itself, however, isn't explicitly political. It's vaguely addressed to a devil-like second person or persons who is bugging Hendrix, messing with his "wife and children", hooking his girlfriend onto drugs, bleeding him dry. It could well have had personal connotations and been addressed to a composite of the various people who had their claws sunk into him, from manager Mike Jeffery to vampish girlfriend Devon Wilson, the subject of "Dolly Dagger" ("stick your dagger into someone else so I can leave . . .")

"Freedom" is also indicative of a Hendrix "back on track" with his African-American brothers, many of whom regarded his stint with the Experience as an aberrant, commercial flirtation with white rock and a betrayal of his R&B roots. "Freedom", for all of its guitar virtuosity and newly acquired studio sophistication, represents a slight return to those roots. Musically, it has a lot in common with contemporary tracks like the Temptations' "Shotgun". The chant that takes it to the outtro, meanwhile, ("Keep on pushin' – straight ahead") is a stirring agit-soul slogan but also says a lot about the musical limitations imposed on Hendrix when he rediscovered a sense of his "blackness". No more of the experimental digressions of his high psychedelic era; now, encouraged by the chants of the Ghetto Fighters, he was supposed to stick to a narrower path of self-expression.

IZABELLA

A Vietnam-inspired number, the dense, humid intro of "Izabella" paints a picture of a G.I. hacking through the foliage of enemy territory in South East Asia. Under fire, he puts out a shout to his girl, Izabella, bids her to "save your love, baby" and promises that soon it'll be her in his arms rather than his machine gun. Technically, you wouldn't have to be anti-war to get off on the vibe of passion and mortal danger with which this song crackles, although the wailing guitar solo ought to be enough to melt the heart of a hawk.

What's more, there's no specific indication that the G.I. narrator himself is against the conflict – indeed, he dedicates his military efforts to his lover ("Girl, I'm fighting this war for the children and you . . ."). Here, the pay-off comes in the concluding, shock powerchord – it's a bullet between the eyes, and the narrator drops dead.

NIGHT BIRD FLYING

"Night Bird Flying" took embryonic form during jam sessions following the *Electric Ladyland* recordings, and was originally entitled "Ships Passing Through The Night". It's one of the tracks for which Hendrix managed to complete a final mix on August 24 1970, and received its first airing at the opening party for Electric Lady studios two days later.

"Night Bird Flying" was re-titled by way of a tribute to Alison Steele, a DJ with New York radio station WNEW, whose nickname was "The Nightbird". It belongs among Hendrix's more mystical songs, in which his love is a free spirit, with whom communion won't just mean a casual shag but a chance to escape the surly and sordid bonds of earth; "Inside your world I want to be". Not that lyrically distinguished, it's essentially a showcase for a winged, overdubbed multi-guitar solo that soars aloft like flock after flock of doves, whitening the sky. It's an indication that whatever else many people felt Hendrix had lost at the time of his death, his playing remained as luminous as ever.

ANGEL

"Angel" achieved widespread popularity when Rod Stewart recorded a cover, which was a hit in 1972. But Hendrix's version, the basic track of which was recorded just four weeks before his death, melts away all contenders. If you have tears to shed . . .

"Angel" had actually been in existence since the latter part of 1967 and, thematically, would have sat neatly alongside "Little Wing" or "One Rainy Wish". It wasn't until the July of 1970, however, that Hendrix returned to dust down the song with the assistance of Billy Cox and Mitch Mitchell and give it another airing.

Hendrix towards the end of his life, the wild, frizzy mane replaced by a clipped Afro hairstyle.

Over a swirling guitar backdrop that drips pure silver and turquoise, Hendrix talks of a visit from an angel, who whispered to him of "the sweet love between the moon and the deep blue sea" – one of his most arrestingly tranquil images. Often, in those songs in which his feminine saviour appears to him, her visits are tantalisingly brief, with Hendrix left wondering when, if ever, they will next occur. Here, however, the angel makes a promise – she will return the next night and spirit Hendrix away, "high over yonder". And so he's borne off, delivering a last, piercingly beautiful chorus, his voice almost breaking under the emotional strain. "Fly on my sweet angel/Forever I'm going to be by your side."

There's no reason to believe that Hendrix chose to rework this three-year-old song just two months prior to his death as a result of any sort of premonition. As fate would have it, however, "Angel" inevitably carries all the power of an elegy or a final ascension. It's certainly heartbreaking in its irony. When Hendrix died, the percussion track had yet to be satisfactorily completed. On October 19, 1970, a month after the death of his friend, Mitch Mitchell went into the studio and completed the final overdubs in what's unsurprisingly been described as an "emotional" posthumous session.

The track is truly moving indeed, especially as the guitars, having hastened into the fadeout, re-emerge one last time, the cymbals rising also in tribute to a crescendo, as if Hendrix and Mitchell have come together for one last embrace.

ROOM FULL OF MIRRORS

Given its debut as a finale in February 1969 at a legendary concert in London's Royal Albert Hall, "Room Full Of Mirrors" sees Hendrix declare war on his own ego. In an original draft, scribbled on Londonderry Hotel headed notepaper, it's the love of a good woman that enables him to break out of his shell of self-regard. In the final version, however, it's Hendrix alone, pulling himself up by his own spiritual bootstraps, who smashes his way to freedom, enabling him to have a clear view of the world and seek out his true destiny.

"Room Full Of Mirrors" began life as a slow blues piece. It wasn't until Hendrix decided to rework the track as a supercharged, state-of-the-art, rapid-fire rock number that it made sense. It's sonically self-descriptive; the way the guitars reverberate, refract and spiral off at echoing tangents is encapsulated in the title. A brilliant studio creation, it's Hendrix still exhibiting the desire and capacity to search at the speed of sound.

DOLLY DAGGER

A raunchy number in the "Foxy Lady" tradition, "Dolly Dagger" is a little skinny and metallic, lacking the raw, sensual booty of that song. It's further evidence that when Hendrix broke away from the Experience to record with a more diverse set of musicians, it did not necessarily result in a more enhanced sound. The efforts of Juma Sultan on percussion and the Ghetto Fighters on backing vocals add little weight here to a recording that Hendrix considered complete prior to his death.

"Dolly Dagger" is the tale of a voracious man-eater with Dracula-like proclivities, a she-devil straight from the old blues nightmares of ball-busting females. It was written for Devon Wilson, Hendrix's long-time girlfriend. A super-groupie who'd been turning tricks since her mid-teens, she was well versed in predating on rock stars prior to meeting Hendrix, with whom she "enjoyed" a mutually addictive, unhealthy relationship. She claimed to have introduced him to acid and, bi-sexual, would procure women for Hendrix and keep some for herself, even indulging in threesomes with Jimi.

A victim of Wilson's charms, Hendrix drew her in with one hand and pushed her away with the other, for she had a fearsome heroin habit. Hendrix had the residual sense to see that if he were to fall in too deep with her, he'd be dragged into smack hell too. Theirs was a volatile and often violent relationship. The line, "better watch out baby, here comes your master", contains in it the ugly, implicit threat of a blow, which Hendrix was known to have made good on with Devon. Typically, she was present in the studio control room when he laid down the actual vocal.

This particular song, however, alludes to an incident when Mick Jagger avenged himself on Hendrix for the near-humiliation he had suffered when Jimi had attempted to steal Marianne Faithfull away from his side. At a party in November 1969, at which both Jagger and Hendrix were present, Jagger accidentally pricked his finger. As the cry went up for someone to fetch a band-aid for the stricken rock'n'roll aristocrat, Wilson at once sprang to Jagger's aid, taking his finger and sucking the blood from it. She later left the party with Jagger, leaving her "master" Hendrix in the lurch. Hence "Dolly Dagger" (Jagger) and reference to drinking "blood from the jagged edge".

Yet if there was animosity between Jagger and Hendrix, the Stone didn't dwell on it in later years. In 1995 he told *Rolling Stone* that he was "quite friendly" with Hendrix, even if he considered him a bit "confused". As for Devon Wilson, she died in 1971, at the Chelsea Hotel in New York (scene

also of the death of Sid Vicious's girlfriend Nancy Spungen) under mysterious circumstances. Some said she OD'd, others that she had fallen from a high window. At the time, she was taking part in a film in which she played the role of a junkie.

EZY RYDER

The film *Easy Rider*, starring Peter Fonda and Denis Hopper as a pair of stoner bikers undertaking a symbolic odyssey across America, was a surprise hit of 1969. Although dated and, to modern audiences, risible in places, it did violently highlight the gulf between the untrammeled lifestyle and visionary idealism of the 1960s refuseniks, and the deeply, viciously reactionary mindset of conservative America. When it grossed $19m, it awoke Hollywood to the counter-culture that had been burgeoning right under its noses since the mid-1960s. The soundtrack featured music from The Band and Steppenwolf, and also "If 6 Was 9" by the Jimi Hendrix Experience.

"Ezy Ryder" was not included on the soundtrack but is Hendrix's own, subsequent take on the movie. Revving up and burning rubber like a Harley

Davidson, it hits a motorik, full-throttle groove, Hendrix's chromium-plated guitar all the sleeker for a novel flanging effect he achieved with engineer Eddie Kramer. The song's hero is a spiritual composite of Hopper and Fonda, "riding down the highway of desire" as if in the hope that once he hits the horizon, he'll simply float into the electric blue yonder, "trying to find his heaven above".

As the hero enters a "cloud of angel dust", the song degenerates lyrically into a garbled mess of non-sequiturs (there's a line about "gotta get the brothers together, and the right to be free" which seems tossed in purely as a sop to his new soul crew). A screeching, quicksilver guitar solo retrieves matters, however, and Hendrix hurtles magnificently onward into the distant fadeout. As is often Hendrix's wont, the sound rears up again; on this occasion, this was due to engineers Eddie Kramer and Kim King both leaning back and simultaneously falling off their chairs in the studio, and, scrambling for the master fader, hitting the tune in the wrong place. Hendrix witnessed the slapstick, laughed his ass off and so decided that the mistake should be left in.

DRIFTING

Another song that reflects Hendrix's affinity to Curtis Mayfield, "Drifting" is pure liquid soul, and was committed to tape following a very short gestation period. The lyrical conceit is a slight but effective one; Hendrix sailing home towards true love, the lifeboat of his Self kept afloat on a necessary sea of teardrops, old heartbreaks and past regrets. With ripples of backward guitars, the gentle brush of Mitch Mitchell's percussion and droplets of vibes added posthumously and tastefully by Buzzy Linhart, this is Hendrix at his most limpid and blissful.

BEGINNINGS

This instrumental exhibited Hendrix's predilection in later years for mellow jamming, especially when playing live. After an agitated opening that hints at heavy musical weather in the offing, it settles into a relaxed, boogie-woogie groove – a little *too* relaxed for some, who felt outings like "Beginnings" were danger signs of a possible lack of focus on Hendrix's part.

129

STEPPING STONE

It's hard to see why this was considered for release as a single in 1970 as it is one of Hendrix's poorest offerings. There is nothing wrong with the playing, as ever – he routinely unleashes an excruciatingly brilliant solo that's dimensions ahead of his contemporaries, but with Hendrix, it's a given that even his worst work would be streaked with magnificence. The song itself, however, is a dull exercise in self-pity. From its opening yee-haw, it scampers along like a posse of outlaws thundering into a sleepy town to paint it red and make nuisances of themselves with the womenfolk. It's lairy: "you're a woman – at least you taste like you are". But when the dust settles, it finds Hendrix morosely resenting the women/groupies who don't offer him true love but get off on his rock star status, only interested in a "ticket to ride", before moving on, like the star-struck sex locusts they are, with Hendrix a mere "stepping stone" along the way.

It is hard to weep bitter tears at Hendrix being sexually exploited by the numerous women with whom he had relationships. However, it's true that,

for all his amorous activities, Hendrix found true love, and the emotional stability and intimacy that come with it, elusive. He had long-term relationships, with Kathy Etchingham for instance, but it was no more possible for the "old ladies" in his life to measure up to the elusive feminine ideals posited by Hendrix in songs like "Little Wing" than it was for them to transform into mermaids.

MY FRIEND

This was recorded much earlier than the remainder of *First Rays*... in March 1968, minus any members of the Experience, in an informal studio jam during the *Electric Ladyland* sessions. Its carousing, ramshackle mood and elaborate, surreal lyrics with their references to pillboxes and pearl-handled neckties are reminiscent of Bob Dylan's *Blonde On Blonde* album, particularly "Leopard-skin Pill-box Hat". It came two months after Hendrix's night in the "Scandinavian jail" to which he alludes in the song.

In the closing months of 1967, Hendrix had been touring non-stop throughout Britain before commencing a European tour in Sweden. It was there, at the Opalen hotel in Gothenburg on January 4, 1968 that months of festering negative energy erupted to the surface. Hendrix deliberately got himself smashed, then proceeded to apply the same treatment to the fixtures and fittings of his hotel room. Working methodically, starting with a couple of ornamental lamps, he then moved onto the chairs, which he hurled out of the window. His tour manager, Gerry Stickells, who was in the next room, rushed in to try and stop him but it took the assistance of Noel Redding to wrestle Jimi to the floor and sit on him.

The Opalen Hotel was the grandest in Gothenburg, patronised by the Swedish royal family, and its management did not take kindly to it being dismantled by a flamboyant, drug-crazed rock musician. Although Chas Chandler offered to make good on the damages there and then, the hotel manager insisted on having Hendrix arrested. An image of a bewildered Hendrix being led away by police flashed around the world's press agencies and Jimi Hendrix's reputation, not generally deserved, as a rock'n'roll hell-raiser, was sealed. The next day he emerged from a night in jail, his demeanor a dishevelled mixture of contrition and amnesia.

With its backdrop of smashed glass, tinkling piano courtesy of a passing-through Stephen Stills and the generally debauched air of musicians hanging out having fun, "My Friend" captures the convivial mood in which Hendrix spent many of his days, rarely without company. Yet it's also a song about loneliness. The friend Hendrix refers to in the title, his only friend, is himself; he "talks, sees, looks and feels like you – and you do just the same as him." For all the innumerable people who met and fraternised with Hendrix, few felt that he allowed them to get really close to him. He was unfailingly polite and well-mannered, but that was only indicative of his formality and reserve. Ultimately, you sense Hendrix was rather disconnected from the world, wheeling about in a universe of his own too far ahead of his time, lacking kindred spirits.

STRAIGHT AHEAD

The second time, this, that Hendrix deploys the phrase "straight ahead" and, much as he hollers himself almost hoarse here, his heart isn't quite in this farrago of tub-thumping, positivist soul slogans. "Everybody is dancing in the street," he whoops, then later, "Send power to the people/Freedom of the soul/ Pass it on, pass it on . . ." And so it goes on, but really, he doth protest too much. It's as if he's trying to talk himself into these platitudes.

They're certainly fine sentiments, hard to disagree with as phrased and, delivered in the right spirit and context, could be genuinely stirring. But they're not what Hendrix is about. When he sings, "the best love to have is the love of life", it's as if he's singing from cue cards (or, even, in that instance, Christmas cards), reluctantly coerced into the sort of cause that John Lennon, for instance, was able to embrace far more whole-heartedly.

The track is rescued by Hendrix's wah-wah, which hollers a sustained, mellifluous assent like a congregant trying to gee-up a novice preacher at a revival meeting. Indeed, this might have worked better as an instrumental.

HEY BABY (NEW RISING SUN)

Hendrix's query to engineer Eddie Kramer, "Is the microphone on?" as well as two fluffed notes some two-and-a-half minutes into this track indicate that it was very much a work in progress, assembled here from various rough takes. It's to all intents and purposes the title track of *First Rays* . . . and encapsulates Hendrix's sanguine frame of mind as he imagined himself to be on the threshold of a bright new dawn in his life.

Again, this optimism comes to him in the form of an angelic female, who appears to him as a visitor from "the land of the new rising sun" and invites him to join him on her crusade to bring peace and balm to a broken world.

The song undulates to one of Hendrix's most tremulous and affecting solos, as if almost quivering with anticipation. He used the same pitch on the instrumental "Pali Gap", the same, tumbling fretboard effects, like glistening showers of manna. Even partially finished, it exudes a pristine glow.

EARTH BLUES

This is another song packed with exhortations to the soul, here with slightly incongruous assistance from Ronnie Spector's backing vocalists, The Ronettes, chiming in with harmonies. There's a more threatening, apocalyptic edge to "Earth Blues" – you'd *better* hope love is the answer… *better* hope it comes before the summer. If "Hey Baby" holds out the sunlit promise of a dawning Age of Aquarius, here Hendrix is more in tune with the dark times, post-Manson, post-Altamont, post-Martin Luther King, in

which imminent clouds of chaos seem to be gathering overhead. He's still holding out on the side of light but it's becoming a matter of urgency. There'll have to be some changes, "a whole lot of re-arranges". The song is a reality check. Hendrix's head may be in the clouds, but his feet are on the pavement. He urges against escaping into drugs as a means of evasion: "Don't get too stoned, remember you're a man."

The convulsive *sturm und drang* of Hendrix's guitar reflects a world in strife, crying out to the Lord for a helping hand. Hendrix feels a great deal more comfortable and convincing here than he does on "Straight Ahead".

ASTRO MAN

This is the comic end, in both senses of the word, of Hendrix's sci-fi predilection. Here, opening with an heroic promise to "save the day", he announces the exploits of Astro Man, a character clearly inspired by the cartoon adventures of Spiderman or even Mighty Mouse. Hendrix isn't entirely in earnest here, we trust, in his disparaging dismissal of Superman as a "faggot" whose aerodynamic capabilities pale in the wake of Astro Man.

Even with a piece of throwaway kid's stuff like this, however, Hendrix can't help putting his genius about, his wah-wah strafing the sky like a spotlight picking out silhouettes of Astro Man as he undertakes his heroic exploits, with bassist Billy Cox and drummer Mitch Mitchell holding down the rhythm on the street below, as if playing the role of the two guys who ask: "Is it a bird? Is it a plane?"

IN FROM THE STORM

Hammered into shape with the extensive assistance of Billy Cox, "In From The Storm" is a brilliant rush of dense, metal blues that outdoes the emergent likes of Led Zeppelin at their own game. Even Hendrix's vocals, never his strongest point, compete creditably with the epic histrionics of a Robert Plant.

Hendrix at Woodstock. Despite exhaustion, he would pull from the fire what many consider his definitive performance.

THE SONG'S RATHER DOWNBEAT FEEL REFLECTED THE DIFFICULTIES HENDRIX WAS EXPERIENCING

Here, Hendrix finds solace in the arms of a lover, following a long period exposed to the raging elements, which are represented by some precipitous stereo panning reminiscent of *Are You Experienced*. Although Jimi claimed to have been "experienced" back in 1967, he had yet to be put through the turbulent, if often exhilarating, experience of rock superstardom. Now, he hoped, that three-year storm was on the point of blowing itself out to be replaced by a new era of placidity.

BELLY BUTTON WINDOW

"Belly Button Window" was ostensibly inspired by the imminent baby expected by Mitch Mitchell and his wife Lynn, imagining the pre-born infant already conscious and staring out at the world from the womb. However, the song's rather downbeat feel reflected the difficulties Hendrix was experiencing when he wrote the song, particularly concerning the building of his new studio, Electric Lady. The idea that his life could be in danger, following local Mafia objections to the location of the studio and the unwelcome attentions it would bring, sent Hendrix into a sullen bout of musical introspection, which touched on a broader feeling of isolation, of "not living today", of not fitting in on this mortal coil. "I'm wondering if they don't want me around . . ." broods the pre-born narrator.

All he sees is a "whole lot of frowns" which are enough to make him contemplate returning back to spirit land, where he has the option of returning down the pre-natal "chute" in some future, more conducive era. He then addresses the parents, promising him that he'll bring grins and sunshine into their lives, but also asking them if they're sure they want to bring him into this sad, sad world. "You've only got 200 days," he reminds them. If this song was meant to be a soft-focus paean to expecting parents, then it's a morbid one, to say the least, effectively asking if they might want to consider an abortion. Clearly, the song has wider implications.

Although only recorded with a basic 4-tracks, "Belly Button Window" benefits greatly from the consequent sparseness and intimacy – you feel like you're there in the womb with the embryonic infant, the squeaky, tiny wah-wah accompaniment signifying the plaintive, wordless voice of the unborn child.

SOUTH SATURN DELTA

Recorded   October 1966 – April 1967 at De Lane Lea,
                 CBS & Olympic Studios.

Produced by Chas Chandler.

Engineered by Dave Siddle, Eddie Kramer and Mike Ross.

Musicians: Jimi Hendrix (lead vocals, backing vocals, guitar,
                 handclaps, piano), Noel Redding (bass, backing
                 vocals), Mitch Mitchell (drums, tambourine, backing
                 vocals, cowbell).

LOOK OVER YONDER

LITTLE WING

HERE HE COMES (LOVER MAN)

SOUTH SATURN DELTA

POWER OF SOUL

MESSAGE TO THE UNIVERSE (MESSAGE TO LOVE)

TAX FREE

ALL ALONG THE WATCHTOWER

THE STARS THAT PLAY WITH LAUGHING SAM'S DICE

MIDNIGHT

SWEET ANGEL (ANGEL)

BLEEDING HEART

PALI GAP

DRIFTER'S ESCAPE

MIDNIGHT LIGHTNING

Following jimi Hendrix's death, his "work in progress" consisting of numerous unfinished tracks and unreleased material, fell into the hands of the producer Alan Douglas and his company Are You Experienced.

Douglas had many contacts in the jazz world through his own label, which he had launched through United Artists. He'd worked with everyone from Duke Ellington to the Last Poets and was impressed by Hendrix's improvisational abilities, following a chance encounter with his music on the radio.

In turn, Douglas had opened up a new avenue of musical speculation to Hendrix, arranging for him to work on both an album and a concert with Gil Evans, who had made big band arrangements for Miles Davis on albums like *Sketches Of Spain*. Hendrix's death tragically precluded his own involvement, though Evans did go ahead and release an album, *The Gil Evans Orchestra Plays The Music Of Jimi Hendrix* which, fine as it was, couldn't quite banish the nagging whisper of "If only . . ."

HENDRIX'S LEGACY WAS NOW BACK IN THE CONTROL OF HIS FAMILY AND THEIR ADVISERS

However, Douglas appalled many in his stewardship of Hendrix's legacy. Posthumous albums such as *Crash Landing* and *Midnight Lightning* featured Hendrix material that was sanitised with the original backing tracks erased and, to the jaw-dropping disgust of Hendrix aficionados, included overdubs from session musicians and even other guitarists. Douglas had intended to "update" the recordings but most considered his efforts presumptuous, even sacrilegious – one interviewer pointing out to him that it was "like remixing the Bible".

Many people close to Hendrix, such as Chas Chandler, withheld tapes of material, determined that Douglas wouldn't get his hands on them.

Al Hendrix. He and step-daughter Janie would only acquire the rights to Hendrix's back catalogue in the mid-Nineties.

Finally, following a lawsuit and the acquisition of Hendrix's back catalogue by MCA/Universal in 1995, Douglas was forced to hand over all the Hendrix material in his possession to Experience Hendrix, a company run by Jimi's father Al and half-sister Janie. Hendrix's legacy was now back in the control of his family and their advisers.

Once this transfer had been made, a slew of releases (and re-releases) followed, with material freshly remastered under the auspices of Hendrix's engineer Eddie Kramer, who was now back in the fold. Following the restoration of *First Rays Of The New Rising Sun* in 1997 came *South Saturn Delta*, in the same year, which brought together a number of loose ends and rare cuts, some of which had only seen the light of day in the dubious form of Douglas productions.

South Saturn Delta contains material spanning Hendrix's entire career. There's an early, instrumental template of "Little Wing" from *Axis: Bold As Love*, which actually bears more of a resemblance to "Angel". It's an illustration of the development process that Hendrix songs often went through, their meaning and impact determined by the musical shape they eventually took. Speaking of "Angel", there's a fragment of a 1967 take of this song, "Sweet Angel", which was only heard in recorded form after Jimi's death. It's an intriguing demo but he doesn't really hit the chorus with feeling, as if it's just a little out of his reach. Chas Chandler's final mix of "All Along

The Watchtower" features here also. Chandler, as previously mentioned, had quit during the making of *Electric Ladyland*, so this version never made the cut but it makes for an interesting game of compare and contrast. Hendrix would go on to add further overdubs, opening up the song, whereas Chandler closes the lid on the track once he feels it's "in the can".

There are instrumentals, too. The idyllic "Pali Gap" is a sound picture of Paradise in soft tones of yellow and gold. There's "Midnight", which later featured on "War Heroes", recorded with Noel Redding and Mitch Mitchell in April 1969. A baleful barrage of metal-blues in the spirit of "Electric Ladyland", it seems first to die away, only to be reactivated by some serious phasing, twisting and spraying liquid nitrogen. There's also "Tax Free", written by Swedish jazz-rock duo Bo Hansson and Jan Carlsson, whose various chord changes Hendrix slaloms through with typical verve.

Most intriguing, however, is the title track. An instrumental, featuring a horn section arranged by Larry Fallon (nobody, it seems, can recall the names of the horn players) it was recorded in May and June of 1968 during the *Electric Ladyland* sessions. Although a little rough and grainy, it represents for some an exciting glimpse at the sort of music Hendrix might have made, had he followed up his big band ambitions.

Or maybe not. Horn sections do not necessarily jazz make. The brass sounds here, clipped and Southern-fried, are more reminiscent of Stax or the J.B. All Stars than of avant-garde jazz. Everyone meanders in ensemble form through the changes, but it's not until Mitch Mitchell rebels with a breakaway drum solo, and Hendrix chases after him as if instinctively, that the track really comes to life. No particular benefit seems to arise from putting Hendrix in a seven-piece, working off a perfunctory horn riff. He seems to play with all the enthusiasm of a chitlin' circuit reunion jam, surely longing to roar off and do his own thing, the way he had done in 1966. Hendrix didn't need manpower to augment his sound; in his case, too many players were liable to just get in his way, and enforce group obligations on him.

Although this track was very much at the work-in-progress stage, it's hard to see how it would have developed into anything vital. Maybe, had Hendrix, Douglas and Gil Evans got it on, they might have improved on this. Maybe if he and Miles Davis had worked together, as planned, they might have produced an earth-shaking, rock-jazz hybrid. This single musical clue, however, suggests that Hendrix's jazz/big band notions would have proven to be too literal a deployment of his jazz skills. Hendrix was jazz, yes, but not a mere team player. He needed to fly free and solo, like Coltrane in his later years; almost any collaboration would only have inhibited him.

LOOK OVER YONDER

Among the last studio recordings made by the Experience, "Look Over Yonder" was recorded in October, 1968. The song had started life in Hendrix's Greenwich Village days, when it was entitled "Mr Bad Luck" and had almost appeared as such on *Axis: Bold As Love*. When they re-recorded it in 1968, it was re-titled "Mr Lost Soul", then, on a 17th take, changed name yet again to "Look Over Yonder". This was the version that would finally appear on the *Rainbow Bridge* album in 1971.

A typically dramatic Hendrix rocker punctuated with aluminium detonations of guitar and a fulsome, gut-spilling solo, the lyrics tell the world-weary tale of a drugs bust. Here come the "blue armoured" cops: "you even bust my guitar strings", puns Jimi, mirthlessly. They discover his "peace pipe" on his girlfriend and, inevitably, come knocking at Hendrix's door. "Now my house is tumbling down," he rues, as layers of guitar descend into a gibbering shambles.

Hendrix was indeed busted on 3 May 1969 in Toronto, where Keith Richards would later, famously, be detained. Richards had been so out of it when he was busted that he'd assumed the arresting officers were minions from the record company come to help him with his luggage. Hendrix was *not* out of it, and realised something was awry when the customs official

A bewildered-looking Jimi Hendrix is busted for drugs possession at the airport in Toronto, Canada.

conferred quietly with his superior, before confronting him with a small bottle of heroin and hashish they'd found nestling on top of clothes in one of his bags. For officers, who'd had rock's decadent aristocracy under surveillance for some time, this was a coup.

It was also a stitch-up. Hendrix was not, at that point, a heroin addict, and certainly not fool enough casually to pack drugs right at the top of his luggage when passing through customs. Who'd planted the stuff? A girlfriend? A well-wisher? The finger of suspicion would later be pointed at elements within his own management, anxious to keep Hendrix in check. Whatever, it was no use protesting. He was arrested on the spot.

Swiftly granted bail, Hendrix took solace in a holiday in Morocco, where he dropped acid and hung out with the Art Ensemble of Chicago, avant-jazzers whose music was heading for the sort of remote frontiers many imagine Hendrix might have eventually sought, had he lived. Many believe this little hiatus, and the aftermath of the bust, concentrated Hendrix's mind and persuaded him to move away from pop/rock superstardom, with all its attendant hassles, indignities and victimisations, onto a more jazz-soulful and serious musical plane.

Hendrix would eventually be cleared unconditionally of all the charges, arguing that the drugs had been a gift from a fan that he had not bothered to inspect. He unctuously assured the judge and jury that he would never touch a single drug again. As with the hotel-smashing incident, the bust only added to his rock'n'roll kudos, but this was no longer what Hendrix wanted. The possibility of a prison sentence hung over him for many months, a black cloud of anxiety and indignation that blighted the precious little time that he had left.

HERE HE COMES (LOVER MAN)

Based originally on B.B. King's "Rock Me Baby", Hendrix makes this song his own with a new lyric and turbo-charged treatment. Recording in 1968 with Noel Redding and Mitch Mitchell, it's a rascally blues caper, with the philandering narrator forced to make a sharp exit from his lover's bed, grab his suitcase and run like hell when her boyfriend returns home sooner than expected.

A live favourite, the song is essentially an excuse for Hendrix to scramble and take off on a frantic and prolonged fretboard workout, screaming through

the octaves as he heads for the horizon and safety from the wrath of the "lover man" whose bed he has been keeping warm. Hendrix pays homage to the blues but, as ever, brings so much more to it than the genre ever conceived itself capable of bearing. Sonically, he doesn't just hitch a ride to the next county – he charters a jumbo jet and threatens the sound barrier.

POWER OF SOUL

Hendrix's later period, in which he was claimed as a soul man, may have resulted in (self) imposed restrictions, but that is not the case here. A studio version of this song, popularised as "Power To Love" by the Band Of Gypsys live, was included, with posthumous overdubs from session musicians, on 1975's *Crash Landing*. This recording is as near as we'll get to an untampered-with version.

Recorded in 1970 with fellow Gypsys Buddy Miles and Billy Cox, its measured, floating bass and clambering chord changes remind a little of Earth, Wind & Fire and the levitating grace of their best, late 1970s work. There are further resemblances to Isaac Hayes and P-Funk.

The chorus is strictly call-and-response stuff, right from the pulpit: "With the power of soul, anything is possible." On the verse, however, Hendrix digresses and mumbles of escaped kites, jellyfish and low-flying aircraft, before falling back into step with the righteous chorus. This soul is in an acid haze.

MESSAGE TO THE UNIVERSE (MESSAGE TO LOVE)

Another track to have featured on *Crash Landing*, presented here in its original, if unfinished form, this version was recorded with Billy Cox and Mitch Mitchell at New York's Hit Factory. Again, Hendrix is in evangelical mode, as he urges us to "find yourself first . . . work hard in your mind . . . prove to the Man that you're as strong as him." A mixture of revolutionary and self-help ethos, it's one of the songs he conceived during the summer of 1969, which he spent living in Shokan, a small, rural village not far from Woodstock, doing a lot of soul-searching of his own. It's only when the guitar solo manages to wriggle free of the slightly stifling, didactic air of the song and set off on its own course that "Message To The Universe . . ." really gets going until, in a blaze of arabesques and a prolonged peal of treble, it's finally gone.

Larry Lee assisted Hendrix here on rhythm guitar, with additional percussion from Juma Sultan and Jerry Velez. Sometimes too many collaborators spoiled the Hendrix broth, but here they enable him to fly solo while taking care of matters on the ground.

THE STARS THAT PLAY WITH LAUGHING SAM'S DICE

Originally the b-side to "Burning Of The Midnight Lamp", "The Stars . . ." sees Hendrix skirt the borders of chaos, as he and the Experience take us on a turbulent "trip", the nature of which can be guessed at in the title. *Laughing Sam's Dice* . . . geddit? This was one of the numbers with which Hendrix practically brought the sky falling in at Monterey. Here it suffers a little from sounding as if it were recorded from the next room, as if the engineers decided that the sublime cacophony the band cook up here might melt the mics if they were set up too close.

Hendrix bids us roll up for a leisure cruise that will take in all the more picturesque features of the cosmos, including the Milky Way. Working the Octavia, the tone pedal devised for him by Roger Mayer, to the max, Hendrix can barely make himself heard above the shrieking din of his own, multi-tracked guitars. Like some harassed flight attendant, he's forced to holler in order to draw attention to various objects of interest out of the left and right windows. At one point, a passenger ill-advisedly opens a door and plunges to his doom. "That's the way it goes," shrugs Hendrix, who was not oblivious to the dangers of drugs.

Although originally recorded in 1967, Eddie Kramer and John Jansen remixed this track in 1972, for inclusion on the 1973 compilation *Loose Ends*.

BLEEDING HEART

Based on the recording of the same name made by Elmore James, Hendrix's version is so radically revised as to be effectively an original. There's a distressed intonation to Hendrix's vocal, as if he's aged 50 years as a result of the tribulations outlined here. The lyric, dwelling as it does on the theme of loneliness, is close to Hendrix's heart. All he needs is a little love and understanding; thanks, however, to the "misunderstanding" of yet another "no good woman", he's left to pine in solitude, the blues calling his name every morning, the willows weeping for him in sympathy.

POWERED BY EARSPLITTING FEEDBACK, SWINGING IN GREAT ARCS FROM ONE SPEAKER TO ANOTHER

The generic blues misogyny apart, "Bleeding Heart" is amply rescued by Hendrix's playing, from the opening wah-wah, deep and brooding, bubbling up as if from a swamp, to the solo accompaniment, screeching like a cat on a rooftop throughout. This is not a final master – it was recorded first at the Record Plant and then Electric Lady Studios in New York in May and June of 1970, with Billy Cox and Mitch Mitchell on bass and drums.

DRIFTER'S ESCAPE

Another cover of a Bob Dylan song, Hendrix doesn't quite transform the original in the way he did "All Along The Watchtower". Indeed, he delivers the song in a strangely mournful key, as if he's attempting an impersonation of Mr Zimmerman. Still, "Drifter's Escape", which didn't quite make the cut for *First Rays Of The New Rising Sun*, speaks volumes about Hendrix and his own existential predicament.

The song tells the story of a drifter who, like Kafka's Josef K, finds himself on trial in a strange town, protesting not only his innocence but also that he's no idea what he's accused of. The seething mob, however, have decided in advance that he is guilty and, to the dismay of the judge,

are crowding in, set to mete out a rough justice of their own if necessary. With things looking bad for the drifter, however, a thunderbolt from Heaven strikes the courthouse and, as the mob kneel in prayer, hoist by their own piety, the drifter makes a run for it.

Hendrix once commented, "If I'm free, that's because I'm always running." He would have identified sorely with the drifter, his guitars effectively issuing a chorus of "amens" and "hallelujahs" throughout the song, although the grinding, almost flatulent note on which the song ends is a bit odd. Recorded in June 1970, this unfinished version differs from the one posthumously remixed by John Jansen, in that it features guitar overdubs mixed by Hendrix and Kramer in August 1970, days before he appeared at the Isle Of Wight festival.

MIDNIGHT LIGHTNING

Working solo here, this March 1970 recording is an uncharacteristically stripped-down and homespun blues outing, its occasional bum note only adding to its country charm. Hendrix plays sitting down, like some old finger-picker out on the porch, accompanying himself with the tapping of his foot. There are no electric firestorms here, merely a playful, mock-authenticity. This was a sketch for what Hendrix planned as a more full-bodied studio outing, accompanied by Cox and Mitchell.

Indeed, all the action here is in the lyrics – Gothic church bells, the flash of bolts across the night sky, illuminating Hendrix and his lover in a fateful moment of ecstatic revelation, either an affirmation of their love or some terrible judgment on them. Who can say what sort of incredible sound painting Jimi Hendrix might have concocted from such material?

THE JIMI HENDRIX EXPERIENCE

Purple Haze

Killing Floor

Foxy Lady

Highway Chile

Hey Joe

Title #3

Third Stone From The Sun

Taking Care of No Business

Here He Comes (Lover Man)

Burning Of The Midnight Lamp

If 6 Was 9

Rock Me Baby

Like A Rolling Stone

Sgt. Pepper's Lonely Hearts Club Band

Burning of the Midnight Lamp

Little Wing

Little Miss Lover

THE Wind Cries Mary

Catfish Blues

Bold As Love

Sweet Angel

Fire

Somewhere

Have You Ever Been (To Electric Ladyland)

Gypsy Eyes

Room Full of Mirrors

Gloria

It's Too Bad

The Star-Spangled Banner

Stone Free

Spanish Castle Magic

Hear My Train A Comin'

Room Full of Mirrors

I Don't Live Today

Little Wing

Red House

Purple Haze

Voodoo Child (Slight Return)

Izabella

Message To Love

Earth Blues

Astro Man

Country Blues

Freedom

Johnny B. Goode

Lover Man

Blue Suede Shoes

Cherokee Mist

Come Down Hard On Me

Hey Baby/In From The Storm

Ezy Ryder

Night Bird Flying

All Along the Watchtower

In From The Storm

Slow Blues

Lavishly packaged in purple velvet hardback, this four-CD edition represented the next (one would hesitate to say final) release of Jimi Hendrix out-takes, rarities, live performances and alternative takes of his best-known songs.

Similar to the Beatles' *Anthology*, it spans his entire career, from the earliest-known live recordings of the Experience in Paris – supporting Johnny Halliday in 1966 and assaulting an audience unfamiliar with Jimi to a voluminous rendition of "Hey Joe" – to "Slow Blues", his very last studio recording.

While not the best starting point for those new to Hendrix, *The Jimi Hendrix Experience* is a marvellous trove for aficionados. Sometimes, the alternative mixes of tracks like "Little Miss Lover" make you long for the familiar, completed articles. Equally as often, in the case of "Purple Haze", for instance, they offer us fresh glimpses of tracks in progress, highlighting layers of sound obscured in the finished versions – a sort of musical autopsy.

There are funny moments, which confirm Chas Chandler's oft-protested assertion that Hendrix was much jollier company than is sometimes thought. We hear the take of "Third Stone From The Sun" in which Hendrix and Chandler's sci-fi dialogue, which features at the beginning of the track, is played at normal speed. Both have difficulty in keeping straight faces,

delivering the corny, stilted dialogue; "I am orbiting around the third planet of a star known as sun". Chandler's flat, Geordie delivery is hopelessly devoid of Darth Vader-like menace. Thanks to the technology of varispeed, however, they were able to use this unpromising material to chilling effect on the final recording. There is also an early version of "Hey Joe" in which a bashful Jimi blanches at the sound of his own singing; "Oh, God! Make the voice lower and the band a little louder, OK?" It would take a while for him to get over this self-consciousness.

There are live extracts from his Monterey set, which was available as a now-deleted album, *Jimi Plays Monterey*. These include "Rock Me Baby", the old B.B. King standard that Hendrix would later change into "Lover Man", as well as a monstrous take on Bob Dylan's "Like A Rolling Stone". There are out-takes also, from his more ill-fated set at the Isle Of Wight, including "In From The Storm" and a crowd-pleasing version of "All Along The Watchtower", though the latter is best heard in its classic form as an immaculate studio creation.

Quite the opposite is the case with "Red House", a live version of which is featured here. Recorded at the San Diego Sports Arena in May 1969 and first made available on *Hendrix In The West*, its CD re-release is long, long overdue. This isn't just the best version of the song Hendrix ever cut: it's arguably the most exquisite piece of blues ever recorded. The original version on *Are You Experienced* is more of a bawdy rib-tickler than a spine-chiller, knocked on the head with the punchline. This performance is over 13 minutes long, with Hendrix's guitar phrasing as garrulously divine as the chatter of angels. Despite the earthy, comic vulgarity of the song, Hendrix's playing here has the quality of a benediction, full of grace. You'd like to think he played this well the night Martin Luther King died. It's one of the pinnacles of his career.

His covers of rock standards, meanwhile, are sensual and highly charged. He rushes through "Sergeant Pepper's Lonely Hearts Club Band" like a dose of electric salts. Paul McCartney had been on hand to see Hendrix premier his version in London, which he commended as "simply incredible". This take was recorded in Stockholm three months later, in September 1967. As for "Johnny B Goode" and "Blue Suede Shoes", both recorded live at Berkeley in May 1970, he puts both of these old rock'n'roll warhorses through such frenetic paces that he practically burns off their hooves. The Experience's version of "Gloria", meanwhile, is a sheer, tumbling waterfall of serrated rock noise, with Jimi introducing a little naughty, spoken word improv at drummer Mitch Mitchell's expense. This track was released as a one-sided single that came as a free bonus item with the 1978 album, *The Essential Jimi Hendrix*.

There are fragments of works in their earliest, roughest drafts, such as "Title # 3", a heavy workout cut during the *Are You Experienced* sessions which might have been worked up into something worthwhile, but instead was put back in the box and left to moulder. The self-descriptive "Cherokee Mist" is a sublime studio jam recorded in June 1974 that eventually develops the embryonic shape of "In From The Storm".

It's fascinating, too, to track the evolutionary progress of certain tracks. A take here of "Have You Ever Been (To Electric Ladyland)" highlights the song in all its raw, silken beauty, and emphasises Hendrix's small but significant musical debt to Curtis Mayfield and the Impressions. There are two versions of "Room Full Of Mirrors", including its earliest incarnation, in August 1968, as a slow, harmonica-drenched blues number. A 1969 version of "Stone Free", recorded with the Experience, is slicker, more bantamweight and mobile than the original, an indication of how their sound had shed some of its earlier, roughhouse tendencies.

Then, there's a take of "Sweet Angel" (later "Angel") on which Hendrix uses a Rhythm Ace, a very basic, early form of drum machine. The soft, mechanical rhythm with which it marks time is quite haunting – the nearest comparison is Timmy Thomas's "Why Can't We Live Together?" – but it also acts as an unintentional harbinger of the whole era of sequencer-driven electro-pop. Hendrix never took any further interest in drum machines, and there are doubtless excellent reasons to be grateful that he didn't. Yet this out-take offers the wispiest hint of how Hendrix might have sounded, had he been born twenty or thirty years later.

Finally, *The Jimi Hendrix Experience* includes a number of new songs and recordings, either previously unreleased or hitherto unavailable on CD, as follows:

KILLING FLOOR

" … *pour la première fois*… Jimi Hendrix!"

This was indeed the first time and this, along with "Hey Joe", taken from the same concert, represents the earliest known recording of the Jimi Hendrix Experience, made before they'd even entered the studio. Following Hendrix's very first British gig, sitting in with Brian Auger and the Oblivion Express at the Blaises club on September 29, 1966, French superstar Johnny Halliday, who had been in attendance, immediately invited him and the Experience to support him in at a series of concerts in France. On October 18, at the Olympia Theatre in Paris, they played to a sellout audience of 14,500.

Even in such large venues, supporting acts can often find themselves faced by deathly indifference and even resentment from punters impatient for the main event. However, Hendrix displayed his entire bag of tricks, including playing his guitar one-handed and playing two guitars at the same time, one with his hands, one with his foot. Hendrix also learned a trick or two from the wings from Halliday as to working an audience, and on this short European tour the band were to quickly formulate an act based on energy, virtuosity and showmanship. They were given a storming reception. Almost a year to the day later, Hendrix would return to the same venue, this time as a star in his own right, and humbly thank the Parisian audience for the welcome they'd given him; "Instead of booing us off the stage, you gave us a chance." Like many a jazzman in the Forties and Fifties, Hendrix had been surprised and touched at the hospitality and attention he'd received in Europe, in contrast to his homeland.

"Killing Floor" was a late 1950s composition by Chicago bluesman Howlin' Wolf, whose life had literally reflected the blues' transition from rural to urban – he had given up the life of a farmer to record blues full-time for the Chess label, only making his recording debut at the age of 40. Born Chester Burnett in 1910, standing 6'6" and weighing 300 pounds, he was a fearsome, primal stage presence, who was able to dominate even an electric band with a growling vocal style drawn from deep in his belly and fierce harmonica broadsides. Idolised by younger electric blues men such as the Rolling Stones, he took the fledgling Hendrix under his wing when Jimi was still trying to earn his spurs in America. According to Johnny Winter, however, Howlin' Wolf was rather cooler with Hendrix when he sat in with him at a later date. "He kind of put him down," recalled Winter. "This bothered Jimi, because Wolf was one of his idols." Wolf, however, resented young bucks like Hendrix who were making a whole lot more money out of the blues than he ever had, simply by adding a few rock'n'roll, modernistic knobs such as feedback.

All of which would have been greatly unfair to Hendrix. He paid homage to the blues but he didn't bastardise them – indeed, he developed them into a great deal more than the usual 1960s blues rocker whose reverence often took the form of plagiarism. Here, in this typical lament against a ball-busting female whose wrongdoings have reduced the blues man to abject tears, he demonstrates a number of his trademark effects, over Mitchell and Redding's rumbling rhythm section, including sizzling guitar vibrato and a twang of feedback on the solo. It's only a hint of what was to come, but by the standards of the day, the Geiger counter reading registered here would have been astounding.

TAKING CARE OF NO BUSINESS

Another blues outing, recorded in May 1967 during the early sessions for *Axis: Bold As Love*, this self-penned composition sees Hendrix very much wearing his comic hat tilted at a rakish edge. In a boisterous studio atmosphere, plucking away in the mock-shambolic manner of a busker, Hendrix plays the role of a bum, drawing on his days of impoverishment as a starving musician in the early 1960s for inspiration.

The track opens with one bit of business – one of Jimi's session cohorts plays the part of a bartender heaving Jimi out. Hendrix then embarks on a series of bluesy couplets which amount at times to a sort of stand-up routine, as he fights with a cat over alley territory, has his sandwich stolen by a rat, and talks about the menial jobs he's had to give up because they involve standing up and "standing up is like dyin'." Hendrix's bum, it turns out, is a victim of his own bone-idleness rather than an unjust society. He lives on in the hope that some "rich fool" will drop him a dime. He'd cry, he says, but "my tears are too lazy to fall down".

This is the Hendrix that didn't often get a public airing – the prankster and arch-impressionist who did a wicked Little Richard, leaving those around him doubled up with laughter.

CATFISH BLUES

Almost a year after his first appearance at the Olympia Theatre, Paris, supporting Johnny Halliday, Hendrix returned and lavished on his appreciative French audience this slow-burning, bluesy take on Muddy Waters' "Mannish Boy", which appears to give birth to the riff that would later be the foundation for "Voodoo Chile".

SOMEWHERE

First aired with controversial session overdubs on the 1975 album *Crash Landing* as "Somewhere Over The Rainbow", this March 1968 demo is the sole surviving version of the song before *Crash Landing* producer Alan Douglas

got his hands on it. Mitch Mitchell added drum parts in 1971. The opening verse, culminating in the plea to the Lord to "give us a helping hand" was raided for "Earth Blues". "Somewhere" develops rather differently. Proceeding at a solemn pace, Olympian and psychedelic, it sees Hendrix speculate about aliens distantly observing humanity from the skies, shaking their heads at our uptightness – "they sure know how to make a mess."

He then reflects on his own lot as a rock commodity – "they try to wrap me in cellophane and sell me." This track very much marks Hendrix's increasing disenchantment with his pop status and the treadmill he was on, as well as his ever-burgeoning, if rather, cloudy social conscience.

IT'S TOO BAD

In stark contrast to "Taking Care Of No Business", "It's Too Bad" is Hendrix at his most sombre and subdued. A slow blues procession recorded in February 1969 with Buddy Miles and organist Larry Young, it finds Hendrix reflecting on his relationship with his brother Leon.

Six years younger than Jimi, Leon was born when father Al and mother Lucille briefly reunited in the late 1940s. He and Jimi were tight as young children but became traumatically separated as Leon was bundled off alone to a series of foster homes, when Jimi ran away to join the army. Photos of

Hendrix (right) with his father Al (centre), brother Leon (left) and step-sister Janie.

Leon, both as a boy and as an adult, show an unsmiling, troubled-looking figure, with Jimi beaming affably by contrast. Leon became a musician himself, playing in a number of funk bands around LA and doing session work from the late 1960s onwards. Hendrix helped him out as best he could but it was inevitably a struggle for Leon to assert his identity in the shadow of his big bro', and he fell into bad habits.

It's clear that they had their difficulties. The previous September, with Leon in jail, Hendrix had refused to visit him. Perhaps this filial betrayal preyed on Hendrix's mind as he worked his way through this unusually reflective number: "It's too bad that my brother can't be here today." Hendrix also alludes to Leon in "Castles Made Of Sand" – he's the proud young brave, yearning to grow into a fierce warrior Indian chief. Leon would have continual problems with drug addiction, later claiming that it had been Jimi who had introduced him to the bad stuff.

Trouble of all kinds has dogged Leon. In April 2002, he filed a lawsuit against his step-sister Janie Hendrix, when he only received a single gold disc by way of inheritance following father Al's death earlier that month. The Hendrix estate had been estimated to be worth $100m. He claimed that Janie had persuaded his father, a simple, gullible man in poor health by his account, to disown him. Janie and her lawyers have hit back, depicted Leon as a lifelong freeloader and addict.

Many hardcore Hendrix devotees incline towards Leon, insofar he is at least a blood-relative to Jimi, whereas Janie was Al's adopted daughter following a second marriage. They also dislike some of the more tacky memorabilia that has been peddled under her stewardship of the estate. Al himself, however, stated in his autobiography that he did not actually believe that Leon was his legitimate son.

Dropping the painful subject of his brother on "It's Too Bad", Hendrix then ruminates on his relationship with the black community and his own feelings of estrangement; "They say, man, until you come back completely black, go back from where you came from too." It's interesting that Hendrix feels free to wax on this topic in the company of two black musicians, Miles and the late Larry Young, who would be associated with his later move in a "blacker" direction. They would have been sympathetic however, to Hendrix's desire not to be defined by his race, and had an innate understanding of the existential difficulties facing African-Americans in the 1960s to which his white counterparts, however much they worshipped him, were oblivious. The interplay between Hendrix and Young is brilliant, evoking the heavy shading of a deep, small hours heart-to-heart conversation. Hendrix and Young would pair up again with equally fruitful results on the now sadly unavailable instrumental album *Nine To The Universe*.

THE STAR-SPANGLED BANNER

It's ironic that Hendrix's most devastating, infamous and eloquent political statement should have come in the form of an instrumental. Then again, Hendrix was rarely explicitly political. Not rebellious by nature, inclined to passivity in the face of his father's discipline, Hendrix was, if anything, initially intrinsically conservative. As an ex-paratrooper, he'd argued well into the Vietnam War that the American involvement was necessary, so as to prevent a "domino effect" of far Eastern states falling into Communist hands. When Eric Burdon argued with him about Vietnam, Hendrix warned him that without US intervention, the entire region would be overrun by hordes of Red Chinese.

Even when he did develop a sense of political indignation, Hendrix preferred to feed any anger he harboured into his music rather than mount a soapbox. It was an escapism of sorts, albeit escapism with a political component. By 1969, however, he could not but be aware of the stormy political climate, of the growing counter-culture around him, and, as a superstar, of his central role within that culture. Indeed, with "The Star-Spangled Banner", he would become its lightning rod.

Hendrix was not the first musician to raise eyebrows with an offbeat rendition of the US national anthem. In 1968, Jose Feliciano had performed a typically slow, bluesy rendition of *The Star-Spangled Banner* before a World Series game in Detroit. That had caused a stir but it was a mere whisper of insolence, if insolence it was at all. When Jimi Hendrix played the anthem at Woodstock on August 17, 1969, it did more than raise eyebrows: it blow-torched them clean off.

This was, unmistakably, a desecration, albeit a magnificent one. Over Mitch Mitchell's melee of new jazz percussion, Hendrix, guitar tuned to maximum scathing, lets loose an excruciating, discordant take on the anthem, dripping and seething with acid sarcasm, a single, maniacal outburst of the suppressed rage which he'd previously taken out on a Gothenburg hotel room. This was more than a symbolic act of flag burning. Here was a Leviathan of 1960s rock ripping the Stars and Stripes from its pole, wiping his huge electric backside with it and hoisting his freak flag aloft in its place. It's a grotesque parody of a nation's distorted sense of patriotism, of a superstate oozing into the mire of its own moral sleaze, a salutary address from the mud of Woodstock to the brown killing fields of Vietnam.

Reactions to this addition to his repertoire were often hostile. The *L.A. Times* accused him of the "cheapest form of sensationalism". When he played Dallas, Hendrix found the way barred to his dressing room by five thugs who told Hendrix if he played "The Star-Spangled Banner" he wouldn't get out of the venue alive. He played it anyway. Others were enraptured. A young P.J.O'Rourke dubbed the performance "the best thing I'd heard since Billie Holiday". Others considered it the single most important rock statement of the 1960s. Said Hendrix himself, "When ["The Star-Spangled Banner"] was written it was . . nice and inspiring, you know? But nowadays, we play it the way the air is in America today. The air is slightly static, isn't it?"

Many thought at the time that Hendrix's rendition of "The Star-Spangled Banner" was a spontaneous gesture. However, he'd debuted it at the Royal Albert Hall back in February, and had gone into the studio and recorded an earlier version in March for unaccompanied guitar. Originally released on the *Rainbow Bridge* soundtrack, it was unavailable on CD until the release of *The Jimi Hendrix Experience* box set.

This version varies markedly from the Woodstock one. Very much a studio-engineered creation, its opening fanfare, a glittering, myriad shower of electric ticker-tape, sounds like it was achieved on some sort of electric organ. In fact, it's Hendrix working his various gadgets. His guitars were

recorded at half-speed so that when played at normal speed they sounded twice as fast. Sound engineer Eddie Kramer was, as ever, amazed at the "variety of tone colours" Hendrix had at his disposal. As with the Woodstock performance however, the track seizes up and takes on a sinister bent as the grinding bass tones kick in and the heat intensifies. It's as if Uncle Sam's waxen flesh has been melted away, revealing him to be a cyberman.

Strangely, the star to have come closest to emulating Hendrix's gesture came from the world of sitcom – Roseanne Barr delivered a deliberately squawking, off-key rendition of "The Star-Spangled Banner" prior to a 1990 baseball game in San Diego, which President George Bush promptly condemned as "disgusting". Faithful Hendrix impersonator Stevie Ray Vaughan did his own electric take on the anthem in 1985 at the opening of the new baseball season in Houston but, as with Bruce Springsteen's "Born In The USA", this turned out to be another example of US rock'n'roll being unironically mistranslated as patriotic fervour during the Reagan years and beyond.

COUNTRY BLUES

A studio take from January 1970, this features Hendrix in a sit-down instrumental jam with fellow Band Of Gypsys members Buddy Miles and Billy Cox. A distant harmonica adds to the front porch ambience of the session, as Hendrix picks off delicious tuna chunks of blues wah-wah, taking full advantage of the easy, deferential groove laid down by Miles and Cox.

COME DOWN ON ME

Another song put through the Alan Douglas mill for *Crash Landing*, this was recorded in July 1970 but was still due a final mix when Hendrix died. A meaty, sensual slab of funk in the tradition of "Little Miss Lover", here is Earth Hendrix as opposed to Space Hendrix, a rocky companion to James Brown's "Sex Machine", perhaps. Like "Dolly Dagger", it's another paean to girlfriend Devon Wilson, the groupie, junkie and dark antithesis to the feminine ideal he espoused in songs like "Angel", whom he was unable to resist sexually, but whom he regarded as a dangerous and malign influence in his life.

There is no mistaking his intentions – he induces a grimace when he sings, "I want you so much I hope I don't break it." Hendrix isn't afraid to muck in down in the rhythm kitchen, chopping out funky links. He once delivered Eric Clapton a friendly ticking-off for failing to recognise the importance of rhythm playing, a discipline which was second nature to him following his R&B days.

LOOSE ENDS & LIVE ALBUMS

Recorded	October 1966 – April 1967 at De Lane Lea, CBS & Olympic Studios.
Produced by	Chas Chandler.
Engineered by	Dave Siddle, Eddie Kramer and Mike Ross.
Musicians:	Jimi Hendrix (lead vocals, backing vocals, guitar, handclaps, piano), Noel Redding (bass, backing vocals), Mitch Mitchell (drums, tambourine, backing vocals, cowbell).

Albums:

WAR HEROES

CRASH LANDING

MIDNIGHT LIGHTNING

NINE TO THE UNIVERSE

RADIO ONE

BLUES

JIMI PLAYS MONTEREY

LIVE AT WINTERLAND

LIVE AT WOODSTOCK

THE ALBERT HALL EXPERIENCE

THE RAINBOW BRIDGE CONCERTS

WILD BLUE ANGEL

As previously mentioned, for many years, following Hendrix's death, his legacy of recorded but unreleased work was in the hands of producer Alan Douglas.

1972's *War Heroes*, later broken up for use on *South Saturn Delta* and *First Rays Of The New Rising Sun*, included tracks like "Izabella" and "Stepping Stone", as well as the incandescent instrumental "Midnight" and negligible frivolities like "Three Little Bears".

At least these out-takes were pretty much in the state Hendrix that had left them. On two further 1975 albums, *Midnight Lightning* and *Crash Landing*, Douglas showed a profane disregard for Hendrix's unfinished work, choosing to bring it up to studio scratch by introducing session musicians, none of whom had been known to Hendrix, to add posthumous overdubs. These included drummer Alan Schwartzberg, better known for his work with Carole Bayer Sager, bassist Bob Babbitt and even, to the utter horror of Hendrix purists, supplementary guitarists to touch up Hendrix's incomplete parts. *Midnight Lightning* features a studio version of sorts of "Machine Gun" as well as a nascent version of "New Rising Sun", but both are a presumptuous betrayal of Hendrix's interests and intentions.

The same can be said for *Crash Landing*, in which Hendrix's early takes of tracks like "Power Of Soul" are only perceptible through the cellophane wrapping of Douglas's production. Douglas used here the same musicians who had worked on Gloria Gaynor's 1974 disco smash "Never Can Say Goodbye". Nonetheless this album was a huge seller, including to Hendrix novices (such as this author, then a schoolboy,) who, oblivious to the small print, assumed these recordings were the "real thing". *Crash Landing* is,

The veteran blues guitarist Albert King, who was a very early influence on the young Jimi Hendrix.

however, redeemed by the inclusion of the Hendrix instrumental "Peace In Mississippi", one of his heaviest, most thermonuclear non-lyrical political statements, as well as "Captain Coconut", spliced together from various takes of the magnificent "New Rising Sun Overture", a great lost instrumental work previously only available on the Douglas compilation *Voodoo Soup*. None of these albums have received a CD release, and they are regarded as heretical volumes by the Hendrix faithful.

Also presently unavailable, more's the pity, is *Nine To The Universe*, a series of 1969 instrumental jams in which Hendrix was joined by the late Larry Young, who has been described as the "Coltrane of the organ". For some, it was proof that Hendrix might well have eventually "graduated" from rock to jazz, though the album is mostly effective for the particular chemistry that exists between these two players, as further demonstrated on "It's Too Bad", later released on the *The Jimi Hendrix Experience* box set.

Douglas also oversaw, and thankfully left untouched, the invaluable *Blues* compilation, released in 1994. This features a rare outing for Hendrix on acoustic guitar, a version of "Hear My Train A-Coming", which he bashes out on a 12-string with a blunt but highly effective technique, as if ripping meaty chunks from the song. Another treat is a take on Muddy Waters' "Mannish Boy" on which Hendrix deploys all of his ground-to-air guitar technology. "Once I Had A Woman", composed by Hendrix, is his gravest blues outing, lamenting a lost love at funereal pace, his guitar solo a prolonged exercise in breast-beating anguish. His "Jelly 282", by contrast, is a jaunty excursion in the "Still Raining, Still Dreaming" mould, his wah-wah vocalisations quipping merrily away. Finally, there's his definitive, eviscerating, 12-minute electric version of "Hear My Train A Comin'".

Radio One, first released in 1989, is principally a collection of Hendrix's BBC Radio sessions between 1967 and 1968, taken from shows such as *Saturday Club*, *Top Gear* and *Alexis Korner's Rhythm & Blues Show*. Although probably for completists only, featuring as it does rougher, alternate versions of tracks like "Stone Free", "Love Or Confusion", "Wait Until Tomorrow" and "Foxy Lady", as well as a guitar-only "Burning Of The Midnight Lamp", it does also feature some fun items. These include an improvised "Radio One Theme", worked up in five spare minutes of studio time, a tear-through of the Beatles' "Day Tripper", on which it was mistakenly believed that John Lennon sidled in to supply backing vocals, and a similarly rowdy "Hound Dog". Hendrix even repays a visit to the old school, with a version of "Drivin' South", a staple of his Curtis Knight Days, which he proceeds, affectionately, to burn to the ground with an inflammatory solo.

Jimi's playing proved to be somewhat disconcerting for the older guard among the BBC engineers. Finally, after a series of takes, one addressed Hendrix from behind the studio glass. "Look, Jimi, I'm terribly sorry but we seem to be getting quite a bit of distortion and feedback, and can't seem to correct it…"

A later, expanded edition of this collection, *The BBC Sessions*, features Hendrix's infamous television appearance on the *Lulu* show, in which he and the Experience cut short a scheduled performance of "Hey Joe", which Jimi dismissed as "rubbish", and launched into an impromptu "Sunshine Of Your Love" by way of tribute to Cream, who had just announced their disbandment. Poor Lulu was left stranded in the wings as, thanks to Hendrix, the live programme overran, resulting in an unprecedented delay to the following BBC news bulletin.

Many of Hendrix's classic and not-so-classic live performances have eluded official release but, year by year, continue to trickle out. *Jimi Plays Monterey* is a document of the legendary live performance that saw him break like a thunderstorm in the US. Footage of this performance, in which Hendrix pulled every trick and device from his locker, playing at maximum volume and intensity, sees him rise like the flames from his guitar above and beyond the times. Jefferson Airplane belong to the 1960s; Hendrix belonged to the ages. The assembled crowd are a picture of mass astonishment, beyond adulation. *Village Voice* wrote, "It was a strange moment for the love generation, aroused by all that violent sexuality into a mesmerised ovation."

Live At Winterland, issued on vinyl in 1987, is middling by Hendrix standards, but at the time of its release was a timely reminder to an emergent new generation steeped in non-heavy metal, particularly indie/avant garde guitar bands like the Pixies and My Bloody Valentine, that Hendrix wasn't merely a cock-rocker but a sonic explorer. The roundhead wing of the punk revolutionaries had deplored Hendrix's "excesses", but by the late 1980s, with left-field rock again beginning to reassert itself, it was increasingly understood that Hendrix's essence was in his excess. Recorded in San Francisco in 1968, it features versions of "Spanish Castle Magic" and "Tax Free" which blow back the ears like doors off their hinges.

Jimi Hendrix Live At Woodstock, issued as a double CD in 1999, is the most complete version yet of his epoch-defining performance that day. Having assembled a collective of musicians under the banner of Gypsys, Suns And Rainbows for the concert (with complaints that their efforts were mixed out of the final recorded version), Hendrix finally took the stage with the rising of the sun, to a reduced audience of a strung-out rump of 60,000. He was labouring on the edge of exhaustion himself, as his semi-coherent links between songs attest. His playing, however, was stratospheric, not just on "The Star-Spangled Banner", but on "Message To Love" and "Hear My Train A Comin'", the tremulous colours from his guitar flooding out in giddy waves. The 13-plus minutes of "Voodoo Chile" is a kerosene-drenched hieroglyphic babble, with Mitch Mitchell giving him more of a run for his money than he was allowed on the recorded version. Hendrix spent every last drop of his energy at Woodstock. Following the concert, he collapsed and slept for three days.

Albert Hall Experience, a two-CD package, marked the final performance of the Jimi Hendrix Experience in the UK in February 1969. Certainly, there are times when Hendrix plays like a man in a hurry, impatient to crack on to the next phase. On "Foxy Lady", he hardly bothers with the vocals, as if to say, you've heard the song a million damn times. On "Wild Thing", he playfully smuggles in melodic fragments of "Strangers In The Night". They played two dates, the first of which is considered by those who saw it to have been a bit off. The much-improved second, however, was recorded and filmed, though the movie has long since been mislaid.

Rock music was in a high state of ebb and flow at that point, with the Who's *Tommy*, Elvis's return, the slow break-up of the Beatles amid a flurry of headline-catching dramas involving marriages and marijuana busts, and the Doors' Jim Morrison being arrested in Miami, charged with "lewd and lascivious behaviour" after he drunkenly exposed himself onstage. The Experience's performance captures all the kinetic energy of those interesting times, not least on their accelerated and amplified version of Cream's "Sunshine Of Your Love". On "Stone Free", Hendrix takes the ball of the

165

original and runs for miles with it, scrambling over hill and dale with the furious, inquisitive determination of a John Coltrane to reach the edge of the known world.

For the live premiere of "Room Full Of Mirrors", so dissimilar from the eventual recorded version it makes *Albert Hall Experience* a required purchase, Hendrix invites onstage Traffic's Dave Mason on guitar, Chris Wood on flute and Rocky Dzidzournou on percussion for an extended and tempestuous jam. At times, it's more reminiscent of 1960s avant-garde noiseniks AMM than rock *per se*. Finally, with "The Star-Spangled Banner" and the now ritual smashing of the amps, Hendrix ensures that the Experience conclude with a spectacular crash. "It was like the end of it, really," said Jim Capaldi, who had also joined Hendrix onstage. "The Experience was over." In fact, they would go on to play further dates in the US, their final gig in Denver broken up by riot police.

Still more comprehensive than *Albert Hall Experience* is *Live Experience*, which properly features the full concert, plus soundchecks, plus a dodgy recording of the not-so-great lost first Albert Hall concert which took place six days earlier.

The Rainbow Bridge Concert, issued in 2002, documents Hendrix's performance with Mitch Mitchell and Billy Cox at Haleakala Crater, Maui, Hawaii on July 30, 1970. This show was to provide footage for the finale to the *Rainbow Bridge Vibratory Sound And Colour Experiment*, a project set up by Hendrix's manager Mike Jeffery. Hendrix had initially been cool on the project, but somehow, as ever, Jeffery managed to twist his arm into participating. (One of Jeffery's associates later claimed Hendrix had been "shanghaied", drugged and bustled over to Hawaii).

The film, happily unavailable, was a shapeless and confused odyssey into the most addled excesses of hippie whimsy, both in its content and in

its making. It follows the journey of actress Pat Hartley from San Diego to Hawaii and the Rainbow Bridge Occult Centre and its spiritual pot of gold. A regular Hollywood film crew were flown in, but the director Chuck Wein would only film when he felt the "vibrations" were right, as well as having the 400 or so assembled audience for the concert sequence arrange themselves according to their zodiac sign or link arms and chant "Om".

Even the credulous and cosmically attuned Hendrix could tell a dog's breakfast when he saw one. He lay low, had his fortune told (he was informed that, in some unexplained twist of genealogy, he was the descendant of both Egyptian and Tibetan royalty) and smoked dope throughout the production, emerging only to perform the full set documented here.

The show, which took place in the vicinity of the island's Olowalu Volcano, was beset by technical difficulties, not helped by the fact that most of the crew were by now as stoned as bats. Only eight of the sixteen channels on the mixing desk were working at any one time and this is reflected on the CD edition. Despite remastering, the recording is of poor quality, as fuzzy as a 1970s transistor radio in places. Yet even under this duress, Hendrix pulls from somewhere some immense performances – the delicious licks of "Lover Man", the treble-heavy "Foxy Lady" and a formidable "In From The Storm", a triumph over chaos.

Finally, *Blue Wild Angel* pulls together at last, across two CDs, Hendrix's final British performance, at the Isle of Wight festival on August 30, 1970. It's an occasion not many Hendrix fans, certainly those who were there on the day, would especially want to relive. At this point, Hendrix was exhausted, strung out and alarmingly underweight in appearance. The festival was a shambles, disabled by conflicts between the organisers and gatecrashing anarchist groups. Having been beaten to the stage by Jethro Tull ("The golden rule of festivals is never to close the show", said Tull's Ian Anderson), Hendrix brought up the rear of the bill in the small hours. In a bad omen, his trousers split just as he was about to take to the stage.

Looking as if he'd been awoken from a deep sleep and reluctantly shoved onstage to perform, a disgruntled Hendrix battled with a dismal sound system, constantly disrupted by the walkie-talkie communications of festival security, his guitar veering out of tune, his feedback failing to feed. On the last weekend of the British summer, the audience were huddled miserably around campfires, struggling to keep warm. Chas Chandler described Hendrix's set as "disastrous". Yet many who witnessed the gig, or hear it decades on, are still bedazzled even by a dysfunctional Hendrix. As Glen Tipton of Judas Priest said, "With Hendrix, even being out of tune was pretty good."

167

VALLEYS OF NEPTUNE

Recorded	May 1967 – June 1987
Produced by	Jimi Hendrix, Chas Chandler
Engineered by	Eddie Kramer, Gary Kellgren, George Chkiantz, Sandy (surname unknown)
Musicians:	Jimi Hendrix (guitar, lead vocals), Noel Redding (bass, backing vocals), Billy Cox (bass), Mitch Mitchell (drums), Juma Sultan (percussion), Rocki Dzidzornu (percussion), Ricky Isaac (drums), Chris Grimes (tambourine), Al Marks (maracas), Roger Chapman, Andy Fairweather Low (backing vocals)

STONE FREE

VALLEYS OF NEPTUNE

BLEEDING HEART

HEAR MY TRAIN A COMIN'

MR BAD LUCK

SUNSHINE OF YOUR LOVE

LOVER MAN

SHIPS PASSING THROUGH THE NIGHT

FIRE

RED HOUSE

LULLABY FOR THE SUMMER

CRYING BLUE RAIN

Following the tempestuous triumphs of 1968 and the extraordinary feat of rock strength and technological wizardry that was *Electric Ladyland*, the opening weeks of 1969 were a somewhat fractious and anti-climactic period for Hendrix. There were no laurels for him to rest on, no immediate opportunity to survey his prospects and his next move from the Olympian heights he had scaled with *Ladyland*. Instead, he was back down to earth, chivvied back out on the road for a European tour, the relatively meagre royalties afforded recording artists in the '60s not allowing for any hiatus. That is a blessing of the era in some respects, and one of the reasons it is so thick with achievement: rock musicians, even the Beatles, felt the need to keep working. However, Hendrix had effectively parted company with his mentor Chas Chandler, while relations with Noel Redding in particular were deteriorating beyond repair. The end of the Experience was clearly nigh but they were still operating as a trio, despite their mutual frustrations.

Chas Chandler. Without his early management, Hendrix's career might never have been launched – however, by 1969, they were unable to continue working together.

At one gig in Gothenburg, Sweden, Hendrix attempted to escape the confines of the onstage guitar sound through a variety of treatments, radically rearranging old songs, playing his instrument not just with his teeth but even his stomach as if in desperation to tease out something new. However, Chas Chandler, looking on, would describe the concert as "dire" and evidence of the schism within the group. Hendrix expressed his dissatisfaction in a radio interview in Stockholm. "I can't play guitar any more the way I want to. I get very frustrated onstage when we play. Every time we come into town, everybody always looks towards us for some kind of answer … it's very hard." Basic onstage problems like a persistently out-of-tune guitar would appear to reduce him to a crumbled heap, while in Berlin the police had to protect the group in a cordon following reports that there would be a riot. There was a feeling, in rock as in the decade at large, that the wheels were coming off.

After a disastrous start, however, a series of gigs at the Royal Albert Hall did see Hendrix finally pull success from the fire. That would in effect be the public swansong for the Experience, but if they had finally come crashing down, it was in a beautiful explosion of shards.

Hendrix at the Royal Albert Hall – the last major hurrah for the original Experience.

Valleys Of Neptune, released in March 2010, represents an attempt to fill in what is considered a "missing link" between *Electric Ladyland* and Hendrix's later forked progress, as leader of the short lived, vaguely Black Power-ish *Band Of Gypsys* and the more Aquarian, visionary *First Rays Of The New Rising Sun*. Recorded in London and New York during the course of 1969, featuring Mitch Mitchell on drums and Noel Redding on bass (until displaced by Billy Cox in the recordings that took place after mid-April), it consists of old tracks reworked, old favourites run through and embryonic versions of songs that would later appear under different titles. It at once feels unfinished, appearing to require more work and development if it is to measure up to the likes of *Ladyland*, but also supremely accomplished, as if Hendrix had reached a point where he could dash off old standards with the casual thoughtlessness of an elbow motion. That is the strength and weakness of this collection – you sense a man wanting some way out of here, away from this too-tight power trio format, away from those hidebound clods who still hollered for "Hey Joe" at gigs, who wanted him trapped in a permanent 1966.

171

Billy Cox, Hendrix's ex-army buddy who supplanted Noel Redding as Hendrix's regular bassist.

All the same, Jimi had become very experienced indeed at doing the whole Experience thing, as opener "Stone Free" attests. The original, the B-side to "Hey Joe", feels like merely the best a fledgling Hendrix and his team could muster in the time and circumstances. This version (which also appears on the *Jimi Hendrix Experience* box set) is far preferable. The riff is reworked in a manner that anticipates Led Zeppelin in some ways, halting, rising and elaborate in its motion as opposed to the primitive, motorik, straight-ahead chug of the original. Hendrix's solo, meanwhile, sees him jump the lights at full throttle, leaving a majestic plume of exhaust fumes in his wake. Only the slightly hesitant outtro lets the version down, as if he were contemplating a right turn into some other tune.

CAST-OFFS BY HENDRIX'S STANDARDS REMAIN GEMS BY ANYONE ELSE'S

"Bleeding Heart", meanwhile, Hendrix's take on the Elmore James blues number which appears on *South Saturn Delta*, feels a little muddy and pedestrian – until, that is, Hendrix solos, twice, both times slipping with casual brilliance into metal firebird mode, flying around the studio in wah-wah coils, leaving his floorbound rhythm section behind. Yet still you feel that this is Hendrix doing no more than stretching his long fingers, working out.

There's a version, too, of another Hendrix blues favourite, "Hear My Train A Comin'", that is far from his definitive one but is nonetheless Hendrix in full and multiple effect, especially when he cuts loose with the solo, initially humming along to his phrases, his guitar whistling, moaning, jangling with clangourous longing and anticipation, changing colour at will. Mitch Mitchell certainly rises to the occasion here, raining down percussion rather than merely holding down the back seat. "Red House" is covered too, the first Hendrix version of which appeared on *Are You Experienced*. Again, this feels like a pretty routine work through, a warming up exercise in some ways, rather than a new mutation sprouting fresh limbs and wings.

"Fire", however, as with "Stone Free", exceeds the original by sheer virtue of cumulative polish and practice over the years. It's a less gristly, more streamlined version, whose solo licks higher, burns deeper, bends and twines in ways unimagined on the debut album. There is even a particularly pleasing bite to Noel Redding's backing vocals.

Valleys Of Neptune was released by Experience Hendrix, the company of which Hendrix's stepsister is President and whose stewardship of his legacy has not always met with the approval of diehard fans. It was the first release under a new worldwide licensing deal with Universal. Critical response to the release was lukewarm in some quarters. Sean Egan, writing for the BBC, described its previously unreleased material as "underwhelming", and regarded this as a cobbled together exercise designed to "throw Sony a

An increasingly
disaffected Noel
Redding found
himself eased out by
Hendrix in 1969.

bone" rather than a genuine disinterment of valuable new material. Certainly, it should not be regarded as a lost, Atlantis-like body of work in Hendrix world. It doesn't amount to that. It feels like the soundtrack of a man in a quandary, casting backwards in the hope of moving forward. However, grumblings of "scraping the bottom of the barrel" should be treated with caution. Hendrix may never have intended for material like this to be released in this form and would have regarded it as studio work in progress. But cast-offs by Hendrix's standards remain gems by anyone else's and there is enough genius, albeit tossed off with almost absent-minded ease, on these recordings to make this a worthy addition to his posthumous discography.

VALLEYS OF NEPTUNE

A fragment of a demo version of this track previously appeared in bootleg form on *Hear My Music* and on a 1990 compilation, *Lifelines*, while tapes exist of run-throughs of the tracks in studio time with Band Of Gypsys; but this is the most finished version yet issued, the upshot of two recording sessions in September 1969 and May 1970. There would be further work on the track but it was never finally mastered.

Putting out to sea on a warm crest of Mitch Mitchell percussion, Hendrix revisits the thematic matter of "1983 ... (A Merman I Should Turn To Be)" and "Bold As Love", in which some sort of return to the ocean, coupled with an earth-tilting catastrophe prove to be sweet redemption for mankind. "I feel the ocean swaying me/washing away all my pains". Speculating that "before ancient Egypt there were moon trips" and that the seabed harbours lost worlds which are due to resurface ("Look out East Coast, you're gonna have a neighbour"), Hendrix goes on to expand on his visions of "sleeping peaks erupting/releasing all hell that will shake the Earth from end to end.

"And this ain't bad news, good news, or any news ... it's just the truth." All of this is a lyrically pointed reminder of the gap between Hendrix's imagined new age, the one he never survived to see, and the more prosaic, complex way the world actually panned out. In a sense, these lush, turquoise, apocalyptic imaginings were all that he himself ever had in the way of a future.

If "Valleys Of Neptune" is a little disappointing, it's in its pedestrian, ambling process, rolling round the fretboard houses to nowhere in particular. It would have required much more radical processing and treatment to match the exquisite variegation of "1983 ...", whose soundboard adventures matched the images it conjured up. This feels almost desultory by comparison, blood and bones in search of some flesh, tone and spirit.

> "AND THIS AIN'T BAD NEWS, GOOD NEWS, OR ANY NEWS ... IT'S JUST THE TRUTH."

MR BAD LUCK

This was an early blueprint for "Look Over Yonder", which first surfaced during the *Axis: Bold As Love* sessions, which Hendrix had performed live way back in 1966 in Greenwich Village and it is as rueful and flippant as its title suggests. In 1987, Chas Chandler invited Mitch Mitchell and Noel Redding to rework their drum and bass parts and these feature here. The eeriness of such posthumous touching up doesn't detract from the good nature of this song, in which Hendrix self-mockingly laments a broken guitar string, and as his house burns down, adds the deadpan commentary, "crackle, crackle, crackle".

SUNSHINE OF YOUR LOVE

The Jimi Hendrix Experience were great friends and admirers of Cream, Eric Clapton and this track in particular. However, their numerous covers of this track are almost humiliatingly superior to the original, which sounds stunted and lethargic by comparison with Hendrix's. He most famously played an impromptu version of it on the *Lulu* TV show in January 1969, overrunning live, to salute the splitting of Cream, but much as he absconded with the programming schedule that evening, he doesn't so much cover "Sunshine Of Your Love" as abduct it. This, recorded a month later, is not the very best version he cut but it is right up there, snatching up the riff and effortlessly haring off on the sort of improvised trip on which John Coltrane took "My Favourite Things", he, Redding and Mitchell taking it over freeways and dirt tracks before slowing right down, like a car running right out of gas and dumping it, oily and dishevelled as if dragged along by the rear bumper, where they first picked it up.

Cream – Hendrix loved them but took their "Sunshine Of Your Love" to places undreamt of by Clapton & co.

175

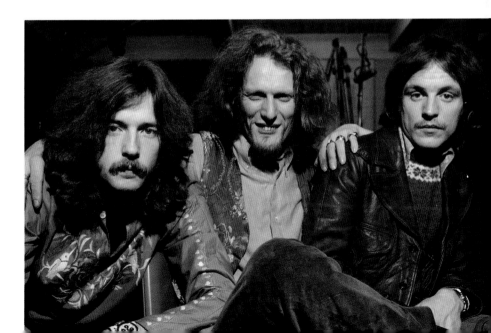

LOVER MAN

Recorded at Olympic Studios, London in February 1969, this was originally based on an old BB King classic, "Rock Me Baby", but was recast by Hendrix who added a whole new lyric from the point of view of a philanderer who catches sight of the partner of the lady he's bedding returning to the house and must contemplate scarpering. It proceeds at a particularly slow tempo in this version, especially given the urgency of the lyric's sentiment, but as Hendrix steps up for the solo he quickly hits a high warp factor – another routinely astounding, astral guitar adventure.

SHIPS PASSING THROUGH THE NIGHT

Various familiar Hendrix themes conflate here – the loner, the drifter, the open sea. On this, what would prove to be the final recording session of the original Jimi Hendrix Experience on April 14 1969, Hendrix fed his guitar through a Leslie Organ speaker, which lends his playing an appropriate nautical glitter. Redding and Mitchell, playing together with Jimi for the last time, create creditably choppy waters as Hendrix solos, his unaccompanied outtro reminiscent of the pyromaniac, vengeful frenzy of the conclusion of "House Burning Down". A pearl this, albeit requiring a little further polish, which has been mystifyingly missing for years since being misplaced on to a work reel in 1974.

LULLABY FOR THE SUMMER

Strictly one for the completists only this – it is instantly recognisable as a rough blueprint for what would eventually become "Ezy Ryder". Hendrix had been kicking this riff around for a couple of years prior to this April 1969 recording, and here can be seen experimenting with the Octavia, the tone control pedal gifted him by his ever-resourceful gadgets wingman Roger Mayer.

CRYING BLUE RAIN

The third song in the trio recorded at the February 1969 session that also yielded "Sunshine Of Your Love" and "Lover Man", this is a somewhat contemplative and subdued blues number, low key by Hendrix's standard. It begins fitfully, like a lighter failing to ignite the first couple of times, before Hendrix vocalises the word "yeah", as if about to sing, only for the song to drift into an instrumental, which proceeds in a series of laconic guitar phrases and hiccups, before eventually breaking into a canter.

EPILOGUE

What might Hendrix have done had he lived? Few among the Dead Rock Star Club excite as much speculation as Hendrix. Stars like Presley and Jim Morrison, for instance, died young but well past their peak.

With Hendrix, there seemed more to come, the nature of which, if his past trajectory of evolution was anything to go by, boggles the imagination. Sketchy works in progress, such as the legendary *Black Gold*, intended as a *Tommy*-style autobiographical rock opera, only hint at where his ambitions might have taken him.

True, there were many who disagreed, who contemplated the grey, drug-wrecked, exhausted figure at the Isle of Wight, jamming pointlessly and drifting up his own fundament, and decided that he was finished.

There were moments when Hendrix agreed. In one of his last interviews with *Melody Maker*, he admitted he couldn't really find a way of adding to the music he'd already made.

However, in the same interview he brightened up, talking of continuing the experiments he'd undertaken at Shokan with a larger number of musicians. "I want a big band," he said, in one of his last interviews. "I mean a big band full of competent musicians that I can conduct and write for. And with the music, we will paint pictures of earth and space." However, Hendrix was at his best when flying solo and dominant, rather than in the company of a large ensemble. There's no particular reason to believe either that he would have excelled as a latter day Duke Ellington figure.

There was also talk of Hendrix and Miles Davis finally getting together, the two great electric jazz and rock geniuses of the day, in an ultimate melding of musical minds. Certainly, they might have made a one-off recording but it's doubtful it would have lived up to its mouth-watering billing. Nor would the partnership have lasted. Most of the great musicians who worked with Miles, from John Coltrane to Herbie Hancock, found they had to leave Davis to develop artistically. For Hendrix to sign up under Miles Davis would probably have meant playing a subordinate role. It would have been a backward step.

It's possible that Hendrix would have been taken with other nascent musical forms like reggae, or made early explorations into African and Asian music, each of which might have inflected and added a new spice to his music.

But while Jimi Hendrix drew on a wide range of styles, there was always a flame-like purity about his sound. Too much eclecticism and mixing and matching of styles might have snuffed out the essence of his fire. Had he taken on these influences in his formative years, it might have been a different story.

And what about synthesizers? Stevie Wonder would conduct his first experiments with them at Hendrix's Electric Lady Studios, and Jimi would undoubtedly have got off on the results. However, Hendrix's special relationship was with the electric guitar, a "technical" instrument in which physical involvement was nonetheless paramount. It suited him perfectly. He was singularly endowed with the gift of creating extraordinary colours and throwing fantastic shapes on the guitar, wrestling with it and wrenching latent sounds from it, kicking and screaming.

However, with synthesizers and such (of which he himself could have taken advantage, had he chosen), the relationship between the musician and the sounds he creates is more remote, especially today in the digital era.

This flamboyant shirt worn onstage by Jimi Hendrix is now a highly regarded – and valuable – museum piece.

Nowadays, sounds aren't physically wrought but juxtaposed in blocks, on screens on PCs. Hendrix would have assembled some fine soundscapes but manual, spontaneous engagement with the tool of his trade was his forte. "My music, my instrument, my sound, my body, are all one in action with my mind," he said. Besides, no one ever actually looked good twiddling knobs or downloading samples.

Most likely, Hendrix would have continued in an essentially rock vein, probably to his frustration, continuing to produce excellent bodies of work but decreasingly at the vanguard of musical progress, before middle age made him something of a museum piece. The 1980s, a decade in which Hendrix's influence was at a relatively low ebb, might have disaffected him for good. As for the twenty-first century, he would have thrilled to switch on his TV and witness the multi-coloured visual cornucopia of freestyle computer-generated graphics which recently formed a fast-moving, liquid accompaniment to his "Third Stone From The Sun" – his oft-expressed dream of a perfect relationship between the production of sound and colour finally realised. Then how hacked off he would have been to realise it was an advert for the new Audi TT, proof positive that his high-tech, futurist visions have led not to liberation of the spirit but to the same old commodification. "Fuck it," he'd probably have said, and retired into private life to play the blues.

Still, as the heat of superstardom gradually came off him, he may at least have found some of the serenity he craved.

What difference did Hendrix make? What did he pave the way for? Well, what's first surprising is one area where he didn't make that much impact. With sporadic exceptions, such as Living Colour or the uninspiring Lenny Kravitz, he didn't open the floodgates for a whole lot of black rock. Sure, Prince played up a guitar storm on "Purple Rain" but Sly Stone provided the real template for Prince. At the time of writing, popular music is, in general, as much divided along racial lines as in the 1960s. Black musicians perform R&B and whites play rock. Crossover has, if anything, receded. But given that rock has arguably just about run its historical course, black indifference to it is immaterial.

Hendrix's legacy is more complex and pervasive. For years after his death, his bequest was considered largely to be a slew of white cock-rockers, who captured the volume but not the content of his work. From faithful if misguided imitators such as Robin Trower and Stevie Ray Vaughan, to outfits like Judas Priest and Def Leppard, it might have seemed that Hendrix's legacy was to blight the landscape with a spawn of bastardisations.

With hindsight, however, it's clear that Hendrix is far, far more than a hippie relic or heavy metal touchstone. His first impact was on the electricification of soul in the early '70s. Stevie Wonder, the Isleys and Curtis Mayfield among others, made the most exciting music of their time after being charged up by Hendrix. The wave of experimentalists who followed in the immediate aftermath of punk also saw past the caricature of Hendrix as a self-indulgent fretboard cock rocker. They appreciated that he had expanded rock's vocabulary, in a way they could pick up on without trying to match his virtuosity or onstage antics. Groups such as PiL and Gang Of Four each contained, in their own way, a spark of Hendrix. Later on, groups like My Bloody Valentine, the Pixies and even Nirvana thrived in the lasting reverberations of Hendrix's guitar detonations. Meanwhile, the entire post-rave/ambient generation owes a huge debt to the "visual" aspect inherent in Hendrix's greatest masterpieces, especially *Electric Ladyland*.

The truth is that any musician with a modicum of curiosity will revere Hendrix like a sun god. There is no anti-Hendrix tendency. He is among rock music's most loved and revered individuals, part of the genre's past, present and future. His music sounds as shockingly torrential now as it did in the '60s. It is still a living, fire-breathing Experience. Henry Rollins said Hendrix was probably rock's only genius, and he was probably right. To paraphrase the poet who knelt before Shakespeare, others abide our question – thou, Astro Man, art free.

CHRONOLOGY

1942

27 November – Johnny Allen Hendrix is born at King County Hospital, Seattle, Washington. Four years later, his father Al changes the son's name to James ("Jimmy") Marshall Hendrix.

1951

17 December – Al and Lucille Hendrix, Jimmy's parents, are finally divorced. Al gets custody of both Jimmy and his younger brother Leon.

1958

2 February – Lucille Hendrix dies of a ruptured spleen, following years of poor health and alcohol abuse. That summer, Jimmy buys his first guitar for $5.

1961

31 May – Jimmy Hendrix joins the 101st US Airborne Division at Ford Ord, California. During his period of service, he meets future Band Of Gypsys bassist Billy Cox.

1962

2 July – Hendrix is honourably discharged from the US Army, having broken his ankle on his 26th parachute jump.

November – Hendrix and Billy Cox play their first recording session, with a local DJ, Bill "Hoss" Allen, in Nashville. The

engineers find Hendrix's playing so discordant that they pull the plugs on him.

1964

March – Hendrix successfully auditions for work with the Isley Brothers, playing and recording with them until the following October.

1965

January – Hendrix joins Little Richard's band full-time, leaving them in June following arguments over pay and Jimi's onstage apparel.

1965

15 October – Having joined Curtis Knight & the Squires, Hendrix signs a contract with Ed Chalpin's PPX Enterprises for a $1 advance, in exchange for exclusive recording rights.

1966

4 July – Linda Keith, then Keith Richards' girlfriend, persuades former Animals bassist Chas Chandler to see "Jimmy James" play at Greenwich Village's Cafe Wha? with his band, the Blue Flames.

24 September – Jimmy and his new manager Chas leave New York for London. Mid-flight, Jimmy Hendrix becomes Jimi.

October – Auditions commence for a drummer for the mooted new band, the Jimi Hendrix

Experience. Noel Redding is confirmed as bassist and Mitch Mitchell as drummer.

29 December – The Experience perform "Hey Joe" on *Top Of The Pops*. It eventually reaches no. 4 in the UK singles charts.

1967

31 March – As "Purple Haze" enters the UK singles charts, the Experience commence a package tour with the Walker Brothers, Engelbert Humperdinck and Cat Stevens. Jimi sets fire to his guitar onstage for the first time.

12 May – The UK release of *Are You Experienced*, which eventually peaks at no.2 in the albums chart.

18 June – Hendrix plays the Monterey Pop Festival, Paul McCartney having recommended him to the organisers. Under the nose of established West Coast rock acts and UK superstars like the Who, the Experience steal the show.

16 July – Jimi and the Experience withdraw from a disastrous US tour with the Monkees, their management fabricating a story that they were pulling out after protests from the Daughters Of The American Revolution

22 September – Ed Chalpin commences legal action against

Hendrix for breach of his 1965 contract with PPX.

1 December – The UK release of second album *Axis: Bold As Love*.

1968

4 January – A drunken Hendrix is arrested in Gothenburg, Sweden, for smashing up his room at the Hotel Opalen and brawling with his band-mates. He is eventually fined the equivalent of $2,500.

5 April – Following the assassination of Martin Luther King the previous night, Hendrix pays his own tribute at a Newark gig with an extended and sadly un-bootlegged improvisation.

May – Chas Chandler quits as Hendrix's producer during the *Electric Ladyland* session, selling his share in the artist's management to co-manager Mike Jeffery later that year.

18 October – "All Along The Watchtower" is released and reaches no. 5 in the UK singles charts.

25 October – The UK release of *Electric Ladyland*, with its controversial sleeve (different from the US version, which was released on September 17) featuring numerous naked women. Many UK outlets refuse to stock the album. An annoyed Hendrix later apologises for the sleeve

1969

4 January – Booked to play UK TV's *Happening For Lulu* show, the Jimi Hendrix Experience famously abandon "Hey Joe" and launch into an impromptu improvisational version of Cream's "Sunshine Of Your Love".

24 February – The Experience play their final British concert at the Royal Albert Hall

3 May – Hendrix is arrested at Toronto airport when customs officers find small amounts of heroin in one of his bags. He is released on $10,000 bail.

2 June – Work commences on Electric Lady Studios, intended as a permanent recording facility for Hendrix

29 June – The last ever gig by the Jimi Hendrix Experience, at Denver Pop Festival. Following an attempted stage invasion, riot police break up the concert.

23 July – Hendrix rents a house in Shokan, New York and begins to jam with new musicians, including ex-army buddy Billy Cox.

18 August – Hendrix plays the Woodstock rock festival, with a band whom he dubs Gypsys Suns And Rainbows.

September – Hendrix is mysteriously "kidnapped" in New York, only to be "rescued" by manager Mike Jeffery.

10 December – Hendrix is acquitted of the Toronto drugs charges.

31 December – The Band Of Gypsys play two concerts at the Fillmore East in New York City. These will provide the material for the Band Of Gypsys album, which Hendrix is contractually obliged to deliver to Ed Chalpin.

1970

28 January – Mike Jeffery fires the Band Of Gypsys' drummer Buddy Miles following the Winter Festival for Peace, during which Hendrix was forced to quit his set after two numbers. Miles claims that Jeffery slipped Hendrix some acid before the show.

12 June – *Band Of Gypsys*, the last album released during Jimi Hendrix's lifetime, is issued in the UK.

30 July – Hendrix plays a concert in Hawaii, which is recorded for the ill-fated Rainbow Bridge Vibratory Colour-Sound Experiment movie project.

30 August – Hendrix plays the Isle of Wight Festival, his last British appearance.

18 September – Hendrix dies, having overdosed on sleeping tablets and choking on his own vomit while staying with girlfriend Monika Dannemann at the Samarkand Hotel, London.

DISCOGRAPHY

Just four albums were issued during Hendrix's lifetime, but scores came out posthumously. For the purposes of brevity (and sanity), excluded from this list are the plethora of recordings Hendrix made prior to his days in the Experience, with Curtis Knight & the Squires and Lonnie Youngblood among others. Some of these were cobbled together and issued during Hendrix's lifetime as spoilers, then following his death as cash-ins. Excluded also are the infamous early 1970s studio recordings made by producer Alan Douglas, including *Crash Landing* and *Midnight Lightning*, which are now unavailable and generally discredited. Further omitted are the numerous compilations and greatest hits albums, as well as bootleg releases – for the latter, the reader is directed towards the exhaustive jimpress magazine/website.

JIMI HENDRIX EXPERIENCE
ARE YOU EXPERIENCED
Hey Joe
Stone Free
Purple Haze
51st Anniversary
The Wind Cries Mary
Highway Chile
Foxy Lady
Manic Depression
Red House
Can You See Me
Love Or Confusion
I Don't Live Today
May This Be Love
Fire
Third Stone From The Sun
Remember
Are You Experienced
UK: May 12, 1967
Track Records
US: August 23, 1967
Reprise

AXIS: BOLD AS LOVE
EXP
Up From The Skies
Spanish Castle Magic
Wait Until Tomorrow
Ain't No Telling

Little Wing
If 6 Was 9
You Got Me Floatin'
Castles Made Of Sand
She's So Fine
One Rainy Wish
Little Miss Lover
Bold As Love
UK: December 1, 1967
Track Records
US: January 10, 1968
Reprise

ELECTRIC LADYLAND
...And The Gods Made Love
Have You Ever Been (To Electric Ladyland)
Crosstown Traffic
Voodoo Chile
Little Miss Strange
Long Hot Summer Night
Come On (Let The Good Times Roll)
Burning Of The Midnight Lamp
Rainy Day, Dream Away
1983. . . (A Merman I Should Turn To Be)
Moon, Turn The Tides ...
Gently, Gently Away
Still Raining, Still Dreaming
House Burning Down
All Along The Watchtower
Voodoo Child (slight return)
UK: October 25, 1968
Track Records
US: September 17, 1968
Polydor

THE BAND OF GYPSYS
BAND OF GYPSYS
Who Knows
Machine Gun
Changes
Power Of Soul
Message To Love
We Gotta Live Together
UK: June 12, 1970
Track Records
US: 25 March, 1970
Capitol

POSTHUMOUS RELEASES

NINE TO THE UNIVERSE
Nine To The Universe
Jimi-Jimmy Jam
Young-Hendrix

Easy Blues
Drone Blues
UK: March 1980
Polydor

BLUES
Hear My Train A Comin'
(acoustic version)
Born Under A Bad Sign
Red House
Catfish Blues
Voodoo Chile Blues
Mannish Boy
Once I Had A Woman
Bleeding Heart
Jelly 292
Electric Church Red House
Hear My Train A Comin'
(electric version)
UK: April 15, 1994
Polydor
US: April 26, 1994
MCA

FIRST RAYS OF THE NEW RISING SUN
Freedom
Izabella
Night Bird Flying
Angel
Room Full Of Mirrors
Dolly Dagger
Ezy Ryder
Drifting
Beginnings
Stepping Stone
My Friend
Straight Ahead
Hey Baby (New Rising Sun)
Earth Blues
Astro Man
In From The Storm
Belly Button Window
UK: April 25, 1997
MCA
US: April 22, 1997
MCA

SOUTH SATURN DELTA
Look Over Yonder
Little Wing
Here He Comes (Lover Man)
South Saturn Delta
Power Of Soul
Message To The Universe
(Message To Love)
Tax Free
All Along The Watchtower
The Stars That Play With

Laughing Sam's Dice Midnight
Sweet Angel (Angel)
Bleeding Heart
Pali Gap
Drifter's Escape
Midnight Lightning
UK: October 27, 1997
MCA
US: October 7, 1997
MCA

THE BBC SESSIONS
CD 1
Foxy Lady
Alexis Korner introduction
Can You Please Crawl Out Your Window?
Rhythm And Blues World Service
(I'm Your) Hoochie Coochie Man
Travelling With the Experience
Drivin' South
Fire
Little Miss Lover
Introducing The Experience
Burning Of The Midnight Lamp
Catfish Blues
Stone Free
Love Or Confusion
Hey Joe
Hound Dog
Drivin' South
Hear My Train A Comin'
CD2
Purple Haze
Killing Floor
Radio One
Wait Until Tomorrow
Day Tripper
Spanish Castle Magic
Jammin'
I Was Made To Love Her
Foxy Lady
Brand New Sound – Jimi Hendrix
Hey Joe (Alternate Take)
Manic Depression
Drivin' South (Alternate Take)
Hear My Train A Comin'
(Alternate Take)
Happening for Lulu – Jimi Hendrix
Voodoo Child (Slight Return)
Lulu introduction – Jimi Hendrix

Hey Joe
Sunshine Of Your Love
UK: June 1, 1998
MCA
US: June 2, 1998
MCA

**THE JIMI HENDRIX
EXPERIENCE – DELUXE**
CD 1
Purple Haze
Killing Floor
Foxy Lady
Highway Chile
Hey Joe
Title #3
Third Stone From The Sun
Taking Care Of No Business
Here He Comes (Lover Man)
Burning Of The Midnight Lamp
If 6 Was 9
Rock Me Baby
Like A Rolling Stone
CD 2
Sgt. Pepper's Lonely Hearts
Club Band
Burning Of The Midnight
Lamp
Little Wing
Little Miss Lover
The Wind Cries Mary
Catfish Blues
Bold as Love
Sweet Angel
Fire
Somewhere
Have You Ever Been (To
Electric Ladyland)
Gypsy Eyes
Room Full of Mirrors
Gloria
It's Too Bad
Star-Spangled Banner
CD 3
Stone Free
Spanish Castle Magic
Hear My Train A Comin'
Room Full of Mirrors
I Don't Live Today
Little Wing
Red House
Purple Haze
Voodoo Child (Slight Return)
Izabella
CD 4
Message To Love
Earth Blues
Astro Man
Country Blues
Freedom
Johnny B. Goode
Lover Man
Blue Suede Shoes
Cherokee Mist
Come Down Hard on Me

Hey Baby/In from the Storm
Ezy Ryder
Night Bird Flying
All Along the Watchtower
In from the Storm
Slow Blues
UK: September 11, 2000
MCA
US: September 12, 2000
MCA

**MARTIN SCORSESE
PRESENTS THE BLUES: JIMI
HENDRIX**
Red House
Voodoo Chile
Come On (Let the Good
Times Roll)
Georgia Blues
Country Blues
Hear My Train a Comin'
It's Too Bad
My Friend
Blue Window
Midnight Lightnin
UK: September 9, 2003
MCA

VALLEYS OF NEPTUNE
Stone Free
Valleys of Neptune
Bleeding Heart
Hear My Train a Comin'
Mr Bad Luck
Sunshine of Your Love
Lover Man
Ships Passing Through The
Night
Fire
Red House
Lullaby For The Summer
Crying Blue Rain
UK: March 9, 2010
Legacy

LIVE ALBUMS

JIMI PLAYS MONTEREY
Killing Floor
Foxy Lady
Like A Rolling Stone
Rock Me Baby
Hey Joe
Can You See Me
The Wind Cries Mary
Purple Haze
Wild Thing
UK: February 1986

LIVE AT WOODSTOCK
CD 1
Introduction
Message To Love
Hear My Train A Comin'
Spanish Castle Magic

Red House
Lover Man
Foxy Lady
Jam Back at the House
CD 2
Izabella
Fire
Voodoo Child (Slight Return)
The Star-Spangled Banner
Purple Haze
Woodstock improvisation
Villanova Junction Blues
Hey Joe
UK: July 12, 1999
MCA
US: July 6, 1999
MCA

THE LAST EXPERIENCE
CD 1
Introduction and Tune-up
Lover Man
Stone Free
Getting My Heart Back
Together Again
I Don't Live Today
Red House
Foxy Lady
Sunshine Of Your Love
Bleeding Heart
CD 2
Fire
Little Wing
Voodoo Chile (Slight
Return)
Room Full Of Mirrors
Announcement and
Tune-up
Purple Haze
Wild Thing
The Star-Spangled Banner
Bleeding Heart
Room Full Of Mirrors (edit)
Hey Joe (soundcheck)
Hound Dog 1 (soundcheck)
Hound Dog 2 (soundcheck)
Hound Dog 3 (soundcheck)
Voodoo Chile (soundcheck)
Getting My Heart Back
Together Again (sound-
check)
CD 3
Tax Free
Fire
Getting My Heart Back
Together Again
Foxy Lady
Red House
Sunshine Of Your Love
Spanish Castle Magic
The Star-Spangled Banner/
Purple Haze
Voodoo Chile
UK: October 2, 2002
MCA

BLUE WILD ANGEL
(The Isle Of Wight Concert)
God Save The Queen
Sgt Pepper's Lonely Heart's
Club Band
Spanish Castle Magic
All Along The Watchtower
Machine Gun
Lover Man
Freedom
Red House
Dolly Dagger
Midnight Lightning
Foxy Lady
Message To Love
Hey Baby (New Rising Sun)
Ezy Rider
Hey Joe
Purple Haze
Voodoo Child (Slight
Return)
In From The Storm
UK: November 11, 2002
Polydor
US: November 12, 2002
MCA

**THE RAINBOW BRIDGE
CONCERT**
Lover Man
Hey Baby (New Rising Sun)
In From The Storm
Message To Love
Foxy Lady
Hear My Train A Comin'
Voodoo Child (Slight
Return)
Fire
Purple Haze
Dolly Dagger
Instrumental
Ezy Ryder
Red House
Freedom
Jam Back At The House
Land Of The New Rising Sun
UK: November 19, 2002
Purple Haze Records

LIVE AT BERKELEY
Introduction
Pass It On (Straight Ahead)
Hey Baby (New Rising Sun)
Lover Man
Stone Free
Hey Joe
I Don't Live Today
Machine Gun
Foxy Lady
The Star Spangled Banner
Purple Haze
Voodoo Child (Slight
Return)
UK: September 16, 2003
MCA

INDEX

The publishers would like to thank the following sources for their kind permission to reproduce the pictures in this book. The page numbers for each of the photographs are listed below, giving the page on which they appear in the book.

Associated Press Images: 54, 93, 94, 106, 119, 121, 122, 138, 180
Corbis: 7, 11, 178
Getty Images: /Michael Ochs Archives: 173, 175; /Redferns: 4, 14, 19, 48, 55, 56, 67, 76, 78, 81, 89, 102, 113, 116, 140, 148, 157, 161, 162, 165, 169, 170, 177, 186–87; /WireImage: 171
Harry Goodwin: 8, 25, 26, 27
London Features International: 53, 83, 153, 166
Mirrorpix: 38, 61
Press Association Images: 37, 101
Retna Pictures: 142
Rex Features: 12, 16–17, 20, 22, 24, 28-29, 41, 43, 47, 50, 70, 73, 84, 110, 128, 133, 137, 150, 154, 158
Star File: 2, 30, 35, 59, 63, 64, 68, 86, 90, 99, 104, 107, 108, 124, 127, 130, 145, 147
TopFoto: 115, 134

Every effort has been made to acknowledge correctly and contact the source and/or copyright holder of each picture and Carlton Books Limited apologises for any unintentional errors or omissions that will be corrected in future editions of this book.